Cha

Based on a true story.

Change Your Life Series: Book 1

An advice book for teens

Written by Alexander J. Kovarovic

This is a raw and unedited version of the book.

About 'Change Your Life'

"Change Your Life" is an advice book for teenagers, college students, children, parents, and teachers that was written to help aid teens as they struggle through some of the most challenging times of their lives. The book was titled "Change Your Life" because it encourages every teenager to change their life into the best form of themselves that they can be. It shows that no matter what you're going through, you can always reach out for help and pick yourself back up. The book includes short pieces of advice on a variety of teen related issues. The book includes heartbreaking and emotional true stories written by the author during the toughest times of his life. Filled with emotion, heartbreak, love, sadness, and helpful tips, this book is recommended for any teenager struggling through life. This book encourages each and every teen reading it to turn their life around so that they'll have a positive, happy, and love filled future. Never give up on yourself, because you can always pick yourself back up and **change your life.**

**Dedicated to Taylor Johnson
1999-2016**

Warning

This book contains material that may not be appropriate for all readers. The book contains strong subject matters including suicide, sexual abuse, self harm, mental illnesses, bullying, eating disorders, abusive relationships, and loss of life. Anyone triggered by these topics should read with caution.

Warning

This book contains language that may not be suitable for all teenagers.

Disclaimer

The information, advice, and resources found in this book is for informative and educational use only and is not intended for use as a diagnostic or treatment tool. All advice found throughout this book was written based on the author's life and may not be used to help all children and teenagers facing difficulties in life.

If you're having an emergency such as a suicide attempt, sexual assault, or child abuse, please stop reading and dial 911.

Table of Contents

Author Biography………………………………9
Message From The Author………………16
Life Story Of The Author…………………17
Introduction…………………………………29
Growing Up Too Soon……………………35
Saving Your Money………………………38
Not Doing Well In School………………40
Choosing A College………………………43
Public Speaking……………………………46
Judging People……………………………49
LGBTQ Community………………………52
Feeling Stressed Out……………………54
Learning To Love Yourself……………57
Not Feeling Good Enough……………62
A Child Of Divorce………………………67
Family Abandonment……………………72
Family Abuse………………………………75
Peer Pressure………………………………79
Cheating In Relationships……………83
Teenage Love………………………………86
Going Through A Breakup……………90
Letting Go Of People……………………93

Losing Someone Due To Suicide..........97
Advice For Every Teenager...................99
Long Distance Relationships................103
Parents Won't Let You Date..................106
Falling In Love…….........……………...111
Pressure To Send Nudes......................114
Abusive Teenage Relationships............118
Sexual Abuse……................................125
Struggling With Parents........................128
Social Media Addictions.......................131
Bullying……………………………....…137
Loneliness……………………….......…162
Depression And Sadness....................164
Eating Disorders……………….......…..172
Self Harming And Cutting.....................180
Relapsing……………………….......….184
Anxiety And Panic Attacks....................186
Suicide And Suicide Attempts..............192
Things Not To Say.........................…..206
Relieving Stress………………….......…211
Getting Help……………………….....…213
Resources………………………......…..215
Final Advice……………………….....….218
Conclusion………………………......…..226

Author Biography

Alexander Joseph Kovarovic is a twenty year old nonprofit executive director, writer, motivational speaker, blogger, suicide prevention advocate, crisis prevention counselor, dating abuse prevention counselor, drug and alcohol intervention counselor, an in training firefighter, and a talented musician. Kovarovic was born and raised in Gloversville, New York and lived there for over seventeen years until he moved forty minutes away to Schenectady, NY which is only ten miles from New York's capital city, Albany. Kovarovic has had a very difficult past dealing with abuse, depression, anxiety, eating disorders, losing friends due to suicide, abusive relationships, bullying, and self esteem issues which led to a suicide attempt during his late teen years.

In early 2016, he was diagnosed with depression and anxiety and he later developed two eating disorders as well. He had been through a lot throughout his first seventeen years of life, and he was put into many situations that most teens wouldn't have to go through in a normal life. This forced him to grow up quickly.

Kovarovic eventually woke up and thought about his life and what he was really trying to do. Knowing that he would end his life if he continued down this path, he attempted to start turning his life around to try and prove to himself that he wasn't a failure and that he was worth living. He eventually did so by helping others.

In mid 2017, he began working hard to turn his life around so he created social media accounts designed to help other teens through the struggles of life and to give advice to teens who needed help. In only a month he received a few thousand followers on each account. He would talk to teens and young adults who were struggling. Most of them were teens who needed to hear advice from someone who's lived what they're living. He became very successful with this and his accounts quickly grew so he could no longer handle all of the messages alone.

Less than a year later, he became a trained crisis intervention and suicide prevention counselor. He became a crisis counselor with the Crisis Text Line and used this training to further his career and mission in preventing suicide in the teenage community.

He has been fortunate enough to have been able to prevent many teen suicides and he's talked to hundreds of teens about stopping their self harming, drug, and/or alcohol addictions. He has also saved multiple lives from immediate danger.

In November of 2017, Kovarovic wrote his very first book to inspire teens. He wants other teenagers to see what he's gone through so they feel inspired to make a change in their own lives. The book is titled "One Life" and is a biography of his life.

In early 2018, after his first book was published, Kovarovic truly found a love for writing. Since then, he's published over 400 blogs, some of which have been featured on a variety of websites and his work has been seen by hundreds of thousands of people across the world.

In February of 2018, he created the National Youth Internet Safety and Cyberbullying Task Force. He created it to help teens in a much larger way than he was already doing. The task force has already had huge success in communities nationwide. The task force has thousands of volunteers and partners across the US.

The National Youth Internet Safety and Cyberbullying Task Force promotes safe online practices for kids, teenagers, and families. It also serves as a catalyst for the prevention of teen suicide, dating abuse, and bullying by offering resources, education, support, and emergency helplines.

Shortly after the task force was created, he created the National DAIT (Dating Abuse Intervention Team) which is a division of the task force that works to help aid teen victims of dating abuse. It also assists in advocating the prevention of teen dating abuse in high schools, middle schools, colleges, and online.

A Message From The Author

During 2018, I spent months writing this book in hopes of helping teens around the world. This book includes small pieces of advice on dozens of various topics to help young teens and young adults through life. Throughout the book I talk about my own personal experiences and how certain things changed my own life. The beginning of the book begins with my personal story. Then I included a rant around today's society and then the book begins with advice on a variety of topics. Throughout the book, you'll learn about me, my past, and my future. I included many personal, embarrassing, and scary life moments to make teenagers feel that someone can understand what they're dealing with. I recommend this book to teens, young adults, parents, teachers, and community leaders. I truly appreciate all of the support I have received over the past several months. It's a blessing to write my very first full length book at only twenty years old. Thank you to everyone who has supported me along this crazy journey thus far in my life.

Alexander J. Kovarovic

My Life Story

What's wrong with me? It's something every teenager wonders from time to time throughout their life. Most people just say "nothing" or "you're perfect just the way you are" when asked that question. Well yes that is true, you are perfect just the way you are, but does hearing that really help you feel better about yourself? No, it doesn't. Hearing things like "it'll get better" or "you'll be okay" are nice to hear, but it can get very annoying especially when things are only getting worse. People are just trying to help you, but in reality if you could just "be happy" wouldn't you? Ahh, that word. "Happiness." What does it mean? Many people wonder the same thing. Happiness could be a puppy, or a new Mustang, or even dating the girl you've had a crush on forever. However to me, happiness means something completely different. Happiness to me is very simple. It's getting through the day as best as I can. Because for some people, making it through the day is a huge accomplishment all on its own.

Childhood. To some people, it's a very special word that shows a time of innocence. However to others like me, it's something you strive to rid your brain from. Here's a little story about mine.

"I don't care." Hurtful isn't it? I grew up feeling that way quite a bit. Not knowing what day I'd cry in my room, just praying for help to get my mind off of how much I hated myself. My mom struggled a lot herself, and my dad tried to help, but it didn't always come across the right way. I didn't really matter to them as much as I should have, but it's okay. You think you're lonely because your friend is busy and can't hang out tonight? Try being lonely everyday. Loneliness is sitting in your room all day. No one texting you. No one seeing you. No one calling you. No one asking how you are. Nothing. Besides school, you have almost no contact with the outside world. Friends were never allowed in my house. In 18 years I had friends over twice. Two times in eleventh grade. But "don't worry it will get better." It didn't get better, it got worse actually. Middle school was no different than grade school, so I won't go into detail.

The constant demeaning, verbal abuse had finally gotten to me in high school. I was screamed at all day and all night at home and in public. I would get up in the morning usually after two or three hours of sleep and have to get ready for school. I tried my very best to not sleep during class, but it got very hard to deal with all of the stress.

Teachers do a lot of work. Kids give them a lot of crap, but most of them do the very best they can. But a lot of teachers just don't get it. They don't understand the stresses of a teenager nowadays. Many days I went home and with all the yelling between my parents, I could rarely ever focus on my school work. So the next day the work wouldn't be done so I started getting a lot of failing grades. So now my grades are really starting to suffer.

Teachers start getting mad and ask where the work is. I'd just say "I'm sorry I forgot" because I was too embarrassed to tell the truth of why it wasn't done. How could I tell my teacher? Would they even understand or care? Now tests become harder and harder, teachers keep pressuring me for work, home is getting worse. I'm becoming so depressed, that I truly had no energy to even sit down to do a math problem. Teachers and friends thought I was just lazy but in reality I seriously couldn't do my work. I tried almost every day to just get something down on my paper, but I just couldn't do it. I had trouble doing my homework, and practicing my trumpet, and going to sports practices, and eventually even getting out of bed was a serious struggle for me. But what can I do? Nothing. I'm just a kid. Why do I have to deal with all of this? What did I do to deserve this?

Eleventh grade ends, I barely passed.

I started twelfth grade with a positive attitude. That quickly changed. The relationship between my parents started to sever. They began fighting a lot and one day it went over the line, and my dad left. But he took me with him. We went to my aunt's house which was an hour away. I stayed there until June. I had to wake up hours earlier to travel to school every day. I had to leave everything. All of my belongings, all my friends, everything. I finally went over the edge and couldn't take it anymore. It really was a horrible senior year for me. I had almost no friends, no support at home, and not much love from anyone. Some people just didn't get it and some really just didn't care. It's hard sometimes for people to understand what's going on, especially when they have been through no emotional trauma in their lives.

Then, one day I woke up to multiple police officers banging on my door while I was staying at my mother's house. I looked out the window and multiple police cars were in front of my house. Why? Well I had become very depressed and suicidal and I had planned on ending my life that day. I sent my guidance counselor at school an email explaining everything and I expected to be gone before she read it. Well for some reason I slept in that day. Honestly, that saved my life. As soon as I woke up, police were there to take me to the emergency room. I then spent over fifteen days in a hospital trying to get better. I had a lot of trouble talking about how I felt and being there was really torturous for me. When I left the hospital, I was worse. I had started to self harm, pretty badly. It released the emotional pain I was being put through. I started to see a therapist after my release from the hospital.

People leave. Its sad, but it happens all the time. Many people promised not to leave but they did. In twenty years, few people have stuck by my side through it all, and hundreds have left. But remember, one is plenty enough. It's *quality not quantity.* Being popular really means nothing in school. People considered me popular when I was younger but what does it matter? They weren't real friends, they all left. Having one true friend means everything.

My parents were in the process of divorcing now and that was tough to go through, while trying to finish your senior year and getting through graduation. But I did fight through it and I passed all my classes and graduated with actually not bad grades.

I've messed up a lot of relationships in my life. I was always so tired, and depressed, and lonely that when someone tried entering my life I'd push them away in fear of being rejected. One thing I've struggled a lot with is insecurities. Everyone is insecure in some form. Maybe you don't like your body, or your voice, maybe you have bad acne, or you just don't like yourself. Everyone is insecure, but some people like me, are insecure about everything to do with themselves. But really, why? You are perfect just the way you are. No one should ever change you, and if they try then exclude them from your life, because they aren't worth it. What you need to do is then find someone who loves you for you and that's it. Don't change because a guy said to, only change because YOU want to because only you can make decisions on yourself.

As fun and excited as dating can be, nothing can beat a good, solid friendship. Have friends you can be yourself around, those are the most healthiest relationships to have. Although insecurities are not something to stress over, sometimes you are made fun of for them. It's awful. Bullying is not okay at all. As bad as bullying is, people that stand by and just watch are just as bad as the bully. I've lost many people to suicide because of bullying. It's sad that you can bully someone so much, that it causes them to want to take their own life. Bullying is disgusting, and instead of being mean, try being nice to someone who is getting bullied. Be their friend. That way both of you will feel better about yourselves.

Don't bully.

Instead, speak out against it and remember, don't be just a bystander. My high school english teacher used quotes on a daily basis and I've really grown to love them as well. Here is one of my all time favorites:

"Pulling someone down will never help you reach the top"
-Anonymous

"If you break a plate on the floor then say sorry, does the plate go back to how it was before? Or does it stay broken?"

Words hurt. Saying sorry can mend a problem, but it's not going to fix bullying. You never know what happens behind closed doors. The kid you're bullying and tormenting may be going through a lot and you're only making it worse for them. The very thing you bully them for maybe the reason they're so insecure and it may be the reason they are up crying every night. Bullying, belittling, and harassment is not acceptable, ever. How would you feel if the person you constantly bullied took their own life? How would it feel to bully someone so much to the point where they cannot take it anymore? You'd feel like an awful person, wouldn't you?

But, bullying is not the only issue among teens.

I see so many people in toxic relationships and I ask myself "why?". Why are you dating them if all they do is hurt you? I understand you love them and maybe you don't know how to leave, but you should never be with someone who doesn't treat you right. If they abuse you in anyway, leave them, just leave. No person should be treated badly. No one deserves it. I know it can be hard to leave a toxic relationship, so if you are getting abused please reach out and get help.

Whether your parent is abusing you or whether it's your boyfriend, it is still abuse and you don't deserve that from them. You deserve the absolute best and remember, you are always worth more than how you feel about yourself. Don't date someone just because you feel that's all you deserve because it isn't. You deserve the best.

I've grown to learn that what other people think is irrelevant. Over the course of my life, I've had so many horrible rumors spread about me and I've had so many lies about me out there. It's scary to have to go through it, because you really never know what people will think.

Unfortunately, it's 2018-2019. People can and do say whatever they want to make themselves look good, and then people will actually believe it. People make up stories, spread lies, and create horrible rumors just to hurt another person, but the worst part of it is all of the people that believe the lies. You all should know that just because something is online does not make it true. You'd be surprised at how many people would totally block you from their life just because they saw a bad Facebook status about you. It's happened to me more than once. It's one of the most anxiety filled things that could happen to you, because it's a feeling that the whole world is against you. It's a feeling that everyone thinks you're a terrible person when you're not.

I only have one thing to say. If you want to create lies about me and spread them, go ahead. If people believe you, then that's on them. But just remember, doing others harm will ALWAYS come back to you in the end.

If they believe lies about you then that's their issue, not yours. Only you know the truth about you, and as they say: "the truth will set you free".

Even if it's your first relationship, you have to realize that you're worth more than that. I didn't realize that for years and it ended up causing me more harm than good. People would use me, abuse me, and take advantage of me, knowing that I wouldn't care because my self esteem was so low at the time.

Throughout my journey so far, I have talked to hundreds of girls about abuse, and about being in an abusive relationship. I'm lucky to be able to help people, as that's all I want to do.

It's sad. Its sad that some people feel the only way to end their pain is to end their life. I've been through a lot of things and I've still made it.

Suicide is never the answer.

As many times as you may hear it, it's true. Take it from someone who knows, you are always stronger than the pain you're enduring. You won't know what an amazing life you might have if you give up too soon. Everyone is beautiful and amazing in their own way and every single person matters. I say to keep fighting and to stop harming yourself. I know how hard it is to stop, trust me, but it'll feel amazing when you are able to. Just take baby steps. You'll get there. No one knows this but last week a girl came to me and asked for help. I didn't really know her, but I talked to her. And before she went to bed she stated to me "thank you Alex, I was planning on not making it till tomorrow, you honestly saved my life, no one has ever just listened to me before without judging me and you have no idea how much that means to me". Back in high school, if I succeeded in taking my own life like I wanted to and tried to, then who would have been there to help her?

Introduction
We Need To Make A Change

As a teenager, life can be extremely stressful. Trying to balance school with family while maintaining a good social life can be very stressful. Unfortunately sometimes this stress can lead to bad decisions, broken hearts, and low self esteem. Teens face difficult decisions everyday and those decisions can sometimes impact the rest of our lives. The present day is very different from the old days. The number one reason to why that is would be social media. Social media can be a huge problem for some kids and teens. It's not the social platforms themselves, but rather the people that use them.

I include a lot of advice and personal stories in this book because I know how it feels to be a teenager and to go through all the things a teenager has to go through. Life throws curveballs at us all the time and sometimes we just aren't ready and prepared to handle them.

Sometimes teenagers don't like listening to adults that try to help because a statement is sometimes made like "adults just don't understand what teens have to go through". I honestly used to feel that way because some adults never seemed to understand the reasoning of why some teens do what they do.

That's one of the reasons behind writing this book. I'm only twenty and I've been through so much in my life. It's easy for me to relate to teens and it's easy to help them. I think that's why so many teenagers come to me for help and for advice. I've had depression. I've had anxiety. I've had eating disorders. I've been abused and I've been through an abusive relationship. Instead of just getting through these things and moving on, I have decided I want to help other teens. Suicide and mental illnesses are not discussed nearly as much as they should be. In twelve years of schooling, we rarely ever learned about suicide or talked about it. It's like that in many schools and colleges. Suicide is one of the leading causes of death among teenagers yet teens don't know what to do when they need help. There is something very wrong with that.

As a society we need to come together to educate ourselves better on these topics before it's too late.

Your friend may be going through things that you don't even know about because they are not sure how to tell you. I'm very good at getting teenagers to open up about their sadness. I can usually tell when someone is sad within five minutes of talking to them or within a couple text messages. That's just the type of person I am. I care about the feelings of others. Many times teens give out signals to their parents and friends that they need help. Unfortunately most of us do not know what these signals are so we have no idea what's really going on with our friend or child. Many teenagers feel much more comfortable talking to their friends than with their parents and that's totally normal. Our friends are the same age as us and they are going through many of the same struggles so it can be easier to let them know what's going on, versus talking to your parents about it.

There is so much hatred in this world and it's hard to avoid it sometimes. Teens get harassed in the store just because their skin is a different color or maybe get bullied in the cafeteria because they identify as gay. There really is no excuse as to why this occurs and there is no good answer as to when it'll ever get better. If they choose to identify a certain way then that's their decision. Now you certainly have the right to feel how you feel about them, but there is no reason to harass them. Being born with colored skin does not make you any different than me or anyone else for that matter. We are all human and we all can be great people if we strive for it. I believe that as Americans we are allowed to believe whatever we want. But with that said, you should not be making others feel bad for what they want to believe in. We have the free choice to make a decision on how we feel about religion, sexual identity, and government. That does not, however, give you the right to go around town making people feel like garbage for what they choose to believe in.

I see so many people trying to solve things with violence. If someone is killed, we react with fighting and burning of our American streets. If a gay kid walks into school, he's beat up for being who he wants to be. If a person of color goes somewhere, they might be beat up or harassed for the color of their skin. When did this happen to our country? Why did it get this way? We are all human and we all are just trying to fit in. What makes you better than them? We are all equal and I don't understand why so many of us have a problem with that. No one's life is perfect. No matter what color skin you have, no matter who you like in the election, and no matter who you are as a person, we still face trouble. And we still go through tough times.

We need to stand together to help each other. To motivate each other. But most importantly, to inspire each other. I'd give the clothes off my back to anyone who needed it just to see someone smile. As a society, so many of us have become so selfish that we don't even know the meaning of life anymore. The meaning of life is not a Ferrari. It's not a house with a pool and a huge closet for all your clothes. It's not about having the latest phone or the latest clothing. Life is about being true to who you really are. If you aren't living life to the fullest then all that stuff is simply just stuff. Money is an amazing thing to have, but it truly doesn't equal happiness. Many people would disagree with me on that, that money can buy off happiness. But in reality it won't. Maybe it'll make you feel better, but money only makes a house, a house. It will never make a house, a home. Love and happiness make a house, a home.

We need to set an example for our future children and for the next generation. Hatred, racism, selfishness, meanness, rudeness, and bullying is not going to get us anywhere. It'll only bring about more crime, more violence, more war, and more innocent people getting harassed for no reason.

To all the teens out there: lead by example, inspire others, give back to your community, help out someone in need of help, and most importantly be kind and respectful to everyone you meet. I tell this to many of the teens that reach out to me: Always be nice to everyone you encounter because you never know what is going on in someone's life. If you are rude and mean to someone then that may cause them to be rude to someone else and it just starts a chain reaction of negativity and hatred. If you are nice to someone or if you help someone out then you might make their day. Now that's one more person who will be out there trying to pay it forward for what you did for them. A simple "how is your day going for you?" can change an awful day around for someone. Don't forget that.

Section 1
Growing Up Too Soon

Most teenagers want to grow up and get to adulthood as quickly as possible, but they don't typically understand what that really entails. Many teenagers are unfortunately forced to grow up due to unforeseen events or situations. Some teens go through their parents' divorce, some with losing a parent or friend, or some with illnesses, house fires, or car accidents. This causes children and teens to have to grow up quickly as they have to deal with adult situations.

If it's at all possible, I advise you not to grow up quicker than you need to. Live your childhood. As you get older, you'll make mistakes and will learn about different things and this will cause you to grow up. Many parents try to shield their children from growing up because they want them to always stay innocent and young. This actually isn't very healthy. If you protect your kids too much, you'll end up hurting them more than helping them. Teenagers need to be able to make mistakes and learn from their mistakes. I'm not saying that teens should be allowed to do what they want by any means, but shielding your children from everything as they're growing up will not help them in the future when they're on their own.

If you're a teenager, take your time. So many teens rush to get out of high school and then suddenly they have no idea what they want to do with their life. As you work your way through high school, try new things, make mistakes, fall down and pick yourself back up, and most importantly keep trying. If you are a teen like I just was and you were forced to grow up quickly, remember that it's never your fault. You can't control what anyone else does. All you can control is your actions.

Adulthood is stressful and it's not something you want to happen right away. Soon you'll have to pay bills, drive a car, take risks, earn money, and work. Stay a kid as long as you can. If you're thirteen, don't try doing things that eighteen year olds are doing just because you want to fit in. It won't make life go any easier, it'll just make you grow up way too soon and then you'll miss out on being a kid.

I think many people don't grow up until they're 21 to 24 years old because they want to party in college and have lots of fun. Other young adults grow up between 18 and 20 years old because they choose to focus on schooling, their career, and a positive social life. I became mature pretty quickly as I never drank, smoked, vaped, did drugs, partied, or stayed out late. I just never felt the urge to do any of those things, even though some of my friends were already doing such things.

Teens and young adults seem to think that they can get away with everything, but the reality is that they really can't. Underage drinking may not seem like a big deal, but it really is. It's a misdemeanor crime in many states. That doesn't really sound very cool to me, does it? I know you think you'll never get caught, but what happens if you do? Don't act stupid and drink, drive, smoke, or do other adult things that teens aren't allowed to do. You never know when you might be caught.

Section 2
Saving Your Money

Everyone loves money and a lot of people love spending it as well, especially teenagers. I was a kid once, I know what it's like. I didn't listen to my mom and I spent all my money anytime I'd get some. She was actually really right about this situation. She always told me to save my money, but I didn't and then once I got older and wanted actual stuff, I had no money to buy anything. All I had was ten thousand toy cars, a thousand lego sets, a bunch of video games, and a million other stupid things that I'd never touch again. It's wrong to tell a child never to buy anything. That's what makes a child a child. However with that being said, I advise anyone between the ages of twelve and seventeen to save their money. I know it's tempting to buy that thing you want now, but tell yourself not to and instead invest in a piggy bank and put a few dollars in there every week. If you put only five dollars in a jar every Friday between your youth years of twelve to seventeen, when you turn eighteen you'll have almost two thousand dollars in saved up cash. That'll be nice for college, a car, or even a new apartment!

It's simple, don't spend all your money. When you get older you'll regret it when you want things that you cannot afford. I know it's hard. You're a teenager, you want all the latest things and you want to spend it all at once on stupid things. That's part of being young. But, save a little bit as you go along with life. I know most of you won't listen to me, but trust me you'll thank me in the long run when you've got money to buy things for school, college, and life.

Section 3
Not Doing Well In School

Let's be honest. School can really suck. The work can be hard, the homework is stressful, there's so much pressure to fit in, and bullying can really take a toll on you. The first thing that always seems to be affected is your grades, and that's okay! Grades are very important for your future and for college, but nothing is more important than your mental health. Mental health is always most important and that's something that some parents and teachers do not understand. When I was going through tough times, my parents and teachers were still very hard on me, even knowing what was going on. A couple didn't even care. They just wanted the work. When I was in the hospital after attempting suicide, there were still many people in my life who really didn't care about me or my health. All they cared about was my school grades. I've missed school from depression, anxiety, and bullying so my grades did start to suffer. In some classes they began suffering very badly. I knew I had to take a break from everything so I took a few days off from school and I took the time to get all my work made up. I got every single paper turned in.

Sometimes taking a break is okay because we are all human and we all reach breaking points. I do not condone skipping school at all and I feel that it is very wrong. However, missing a few days a year to just take a break from stress and the atmosphere is okay. If you get caught behind on school work, the first thing to do is not panic. It can be scary as deadlines approach and you have to turn your work in. But, calm down. Stressing out and panicking will not help you get the work done any faster. Get a good night's rest and wake up ready to get the work done. Take a weekend and just stay home and finish the owed work. Take lots of breaks and work at a slow pace. Don't try to rush through everything just to get it done so you can hang out with your friends. If you rush, you won't be doing the best you can do, so your grades most likely won't be as good as they can be.

We all aren't the same. This is very important. We all have strengths and we all have our weaknesses. Don't make fun of or harass others for their grades. Some of us are better in school than others. Some of us are better test takers than others and that is totally okay. I was a terrible test taker. I could ace all the work, projects, and quizzes, and even know and study all of the material and still get a 40% on a test. That's how I was in school and I hated it. I used to use flashcards to remember things and that actually did help my grades a little bit though.

One thing I cannot stand is when you are in class and everyone starts asking you "what did you get on that test, show me". I hate this. It isn't your business so keep it to yourself. If you want to show your friends then go ahead, but don't force it out of someone.

I hate seeing people drop out of school, especially because I know they can do it. Don't give up just to take the easy way out of the situation.

To all you seniors out there, congratulations! You made it! I'm very proud of you all and you should be very proud of yourself. I wish you the best of luck in college or in whatever you choose to do next. Remember, you do you, and don't settle for anything less than what you deserve.

Section 4
Choosing A College

College is stressful, so it's only imaginable that picking a college is equally as stressful. Start searching for colleges early. I started when I was in ninth grade. I would recommend having a list of possible options by the beginning of eleventh grade. The list may change, but it's good to have a general idea early on. Make sure to do your research! Look for the exact campus location, classes, class sizes, campus life, teachers, sports, music, security, and everything else. If you're a star soccer player, you obviously don't want to pick a school with a crappy soccer program, the same goes for academic classes. See what the college is known for. Every college is known for a certain program or class because of how rare and how awesome it is.

Make sure you decide where you will be living. If you live with your family then you won't have to worry about this at all but if you are moving on campus then you might want to learn more about the campus life.

Take a tour of their dorms to see if it's something you might like. Also, you might want to think about what distance you want to be from home. Do you want to be less than an hour away from home, or would you rather be as far away as possible? Something to think about. Another main thing to think about is the cost. Community colleges are great, and can save you a lot of money so I'd definitely recommend that. But, if you have your heart set on a four year school, make sure you love it because you will be stuck there for a while, especially if you will be living on campus. Also, think about scholarships. See if you can find a list of the scholarships that were given last year so you can get a head start on what you might want to apply for. Always talk to your guidance counselor as they're the best person to discuss college with!

Also, make sure you choose what you want to do. I know you're feeling pressure. College is tough. You may be separated from your family or your boyfriend/girlfriend and that's hard to handle sometimes. Don't do what other people want you to do. College is your time to shine and it's time for you to let your wings fly and be independent. It's time for you to create your future. Choose the college, major, and where you want to live based on what you feel is best for *your* future.

Last but not least, it is okay not to know. It's okay not to know what you want to do. It happens to a lot of people. At the last possible minute (literally the last possible day), I decided to go to firefighter and emergency medical services school instead of choosing a college major. People judged me, but who cares? You'll find what you want to do.

Have patience, take your time, and do lots of research!

Section 5
Public Speaking

This is something I've struggled a lot with throughout high school, so I understand and can relate well to this. Some of us have a huge fear of speaking in front of others, especially in a classroom setting. I do have a couple thoughts on how to get through this. A couple of these ideas have worked for me in the past.

For starters, you could always talk to your teacher. Go up to them in private and explain how anxious you get while speaking in front of others and tell your teacher you're really uncomfortable with it. They may come up with another way for you to get through your project/speech. They might also say that you still have to present in front of the class. It's stressful, but sometimes we have to speak in front of other people, even if we are really scared to do so. In this case, the best way to get through it is by practicing. Practicing makes perfect, right? Sit down and think about what you want to say and maybe even write it down so you can memorize it. Give the speech to your family and friends before you have to give the speech to your class. That way you will feel a lot more prepared.

On the day of your speech/project make sure to speak clearly. This is most important. The teacher and other students have to know what you are saying. If not, they might ask you to present again which would be an awful thing to have to do. I was always scared to make eye contact, so I never did and that's totally okay! When I had to present in class I usually would just look directly at my teacher and not my peers, or I would make eye contact with an object in the class. Making eye contact with people you don't really know can be a scary thing to do, especially if you have a form of social anxiety which I have. If you practice the speech, memorize it, and find something to make eye contact with then you should be able to get through it a little easier. You will feel very anxious before your name is called to speak and that's normal. I would be extremely anxious on the day we would have to present something in front of the class. I would get no sleep, I wouldn't be able to eat, and I would have panic attacks all day. But, once I got up there and got it over with I was fine. As soon as you get up there and get talking it'll be over before you even know it. And remember, we all make mistakes.

We all freeze up and forget what we were saying. It happens to the best of us and that's okay. Your teacher will understand and when you're done make sure you are proud of yourself for what you just did. Just standing up there and talking was a huge accomplishment that many people struggle with everyday. Focus on the material you are presenting, don't focus on the audience that is there.

I went from being terrified of speaking to a class of twenty kids to being a motivational school speaker. It takes bravery, courage, and practice to learn how to be comfortable in front of other people, especially in high school.

Section 6
Judging People

I really dislike people that judge other people. If you aren't in their shoes, why judge them? Take someone who is homeless for example. Everyone is quick to say that they should get a job or a life, but no one really knows their story. Maybe they're a veteran who came back and didn't have a family or a place to say. It's not okay to judge people and it typically makes you look bad.

So many teenagers judge each other for what they look like, what they wear, what phone they have, and who they're dating. It's NEVER okay to judge someone else because they don't have lots of money, nice clothes, or a car. How do you think they feel? I didn't get a phone until I was around seventeen and even then, all I had was a basic call only tracfone. I used to get picked on quite a bit and I got to the point where I was even scared to take it out in school because I knew someone would laugh at me and judge me because I didn't have the latest iPhone. It used to hurt my feelings. I always thought that I couldn't fit it. Why treat another kid like that? It wasn't my fault that I had that phone and I didn't do anything wrong to get treated like that.

I remember one time in middle school I got a detention for forgetting my homework at home and I was having a bad day so I cried in class. For weeks, I was called a crybaby and I was picked on everytime I had to hand my homework in because kids thought I would cry again. It's little things like this that may seem harmless and stupid, but to some kids that may have been a rough day and maybe they just couldn't handle it so they cried. Don't judge without knowing the full story.

A lot of teenagers subconsciously believe that they are better than who they're judging so they judge them to make themselves feel better about themselves. Many teens feel like if they put people down then it'll make them feel better about themselves because they'll feel like they're better than the other person.

A lot of teens also judge because they see people different than them as people beneath them. Often times, teens don't want to learn about different ways to live life so they just judge. There is a story behind every person you meet and there is always a reason why they are the way they are.

Do not judge a book based on its cover and never, ever judge someone just because of what you've heard about them from people you don't even know. Only they know who they really are. The rumors you hear about people are 85% of the time false. So don't make any conclusions or judgement based on what you hear from people you don't know. Instead, get to know the person and see who they really are deep down past all the things on the outside.

Section 7
LGBTQ Community

I am not part of the LGBTQ community in any way, however I am a huge supporter to anyone who may be a part of this community of people. My feelings on this have never changed. I feel that you should be able to date and fall in love with whoever you want to fall in love with. I see so many people harassing and being rude to people in the LGBTQ community and I cannot stand it. Many people feel that it's wrong and it's totally fine to form your own opinion, but keep it to yourself. We all are entitled to our own opinions and that's just a part of life. However, there is no reason to harass and pick on someone just because they have a different sexual orientation than you. In reality if John is dating Mike and they decide to get married, why do you need to send hate comments and harass them? Are they really going to affect you in any way? No, they won't.

I see so many parents disown their kids because of it and so many families get torn apart because of it and it's honestly sad. I mean it has to be hard enough just telling your family, then to have them disown you makes it even worse. By no means do you need to support them. You can feel however you want, but please have some respect. They are just trying to live their life as happy and successful as they can make it, just like the rest of us. So before you want to hate on or make fun of someone of the LGBTQ community, remember this. They are people too. They have the same feelings we do. They get hurt just like we do. Words hurt.

Let them live their lives and keep your opinions in your own house. There is no reason to go out of your way just to send them hate for being who they are. Try putting yourself in their shoes. How would you feel if everywhere you went people were hating you and judging you just because of who you are?

The Trevor Project
1-866-488-7386
https://www.thetrevorproject.org

Section 8
Feeling Stressed Out

It's simple. We all go through stress and it's just a part of life. It's something we all have to work through. Sometimes stress can cause people to make bad choices and then other lives could be affected. It's important to work through your stress before it gets to that point. No one really has a one hundred percent stress free life. Some may have very minimal stress where it doesn't even affect them, while others can have a large amount of stress which makes going day to day very difficult. Stress can cause someone to do many different things, things they wouldn't normally do in their life. People deal with stress in many different ways. Some people like myself write and listen to music. Others go for jogs or runs. Others work out. Some people even take long car rides or vacations to destress. If you're having a stressful day then it's very important to take a break. It's that simple.

Pushing through stress which results in adding more stress on top is not healthy for you and it might cause you to become depressed or maybe even lose sleep. The first thing I always say to people who are stressed is to try writing. Even if you don't like it or aren't good at it, just try it. In twelfth grade english class I learned that writing is a great stress reliever, even if you aren't good at it. Another great stress reliever is music. Many teenagers use this to get through rough times and it really does work well. Taking a ten minute break to listen to music can help boost your mood and can help you through times of stress or panic. Make sure you allow yourself some free time to relax and take it easy. One of the biggest sources of stress is from being too busy. Make sure you get lots of sleep. Dealing with stress is bad enough as it is, but dealing with stress while being tired is even worse. Even if you have to work on an important college paper, make sure you get at least a couple hours of sleep. Trust me. You'll feel better if you do.

I used to handle stress terribly. I would handle stress in a way that was very dangerous for myself. I'd keep all of my stress inside until I couldn't handle it anymore and then I'd end up hurting myself. You have to talk your stress out with someone whether it be a friend, parent, or counselor. That's key in relieving stress. Sometimes talking to a friend or parent can let you release steam, which will help you through stress in the long run.

Also remember, if you think your friend or family member may be stressed, just talk to them. Take it easy on them as they already are going through enough as it is. Don't add any more stress. If they want to be left alone, let them be. Sometimes teens like being alone. Sometimes I'm like that. Sitting alone can relieve a lot of stress. So don't pressure your friend to go to a party or out somewhere. Sometimes we all like our alone time.

"Do the best you can one day at a time."

Section 9
Learning To Love Yourself

I have struggled with learning to love myself for years and to this day, I think this is still my biggest issue. I have confidence in myself, but there's always something in the back of my mind that tells me that i'm just not good enough. Sometimes I may act cocky, but deep down I'm telling myself that I'm really just not good enough. I'm always whispering to myself that other people are better and that other people can do certain things better than I can.

I think it's even harder for teenagers and young adults because we have all this added pressure to fit in and be 'popular'. People compliment me everyday and I try my very best to agree, but sometimes I just don't. I just have it in my mind that I'm not as good as everyone else and it's difficult to get rid of that mentality once you feel that way about yourself.

I have gotten a lot better with it though. I can take compliments and feel good about myself and I have even taught myself how to handle criticism without hating myself for it. I used to handle criticism very badly. I would have anxiety attacks and become depressed every time someone was telling me that I was doing something wrong. It would get to the point where if someone even told me that I could improve on something, I'd want to give up and I'd start to hate myself and I always made myself feel like a failure in everything that I did. I'll be honest, I still do that sometimes. I have grown a lot, but I'm just one of those people that is always trying to impress everyone so I struggle to take criticism without feeling like a failure. If you're like that, I promise it'll get better. It doesn't make you a bad person, and you are never a failure. You just try to make everyone happy and sometimes that can be a very hard thing to do. You will never make everyone happy and that's something that you'll have to learn like I did. Even if you do everything right, someone will still get mad at you over something. Don't cave into those people. Always try your best and that's all that you can ever ask of yourself.

We should all love ourselves because we are all perfect in our own way. We all have a special talent that sets us apart from everyone else and we're all our own person. No one can be me, and that's what makes me so special. Just because you fail or mess up does not mean that you are a failure. We all fail every single day. That's what makes us human. We fail, we realize our mistakes, and we get right back up on our feet and try it again.

It can take a very long time to truly accept who you are and to truly love who you are. When I met my girlfriend, I would constantly ask myself why she'd want me. I thought I wasn't deserving of anyone and I always felt like I wasn't good enough for a girl to want to put effort into me. I still feel the same way certain days. Sometimes I wake up, look in the mirror, and wonder why anyone would ever choose to love me.

Eventually you start to realize that everyone has flaws because no one is perfect. You may dislike yourself, but everyone hates things about themselves. You may be scared to talk to your crush because you feel you aren't worth it, but I bet they are feeling the same way about certain qualities of themselves. Everyone is insecure about something, whether it be looks or their personality. Focus on all the things amazing about yourself. I guarantee there is a lot.

Take it one day at a time. Try finding things that you like about yourself. Maybe your eyes, or your hair, or how kind you are to other people. We all have good traits even if we refuse to see them. No one is perfect and we all have our imperfections. But, all the little imperfections are what makes us perfect just the way we are. You're you for a reason, embrace it and love it.

I suggest that every week you write down ten things you like about yourself and keep them all in a journal. By the end of the year, you'll have hundreds of great things you like about yourself. It can be as simple as your choice of nail polish, your hair color, or how you helped an old lady that day at the supermarket.

Examples:
- I like the fact that on Monday I went out of my way to help an older man take his garbage out while I was on a run.
- I like that I ate a full meal today, even though I was feeling a bit insecure about my weight.
- I like how my outfit turned out today.
- I like my smile. A lot of people compliment me for it.

- Everyone tells me I'm really funny and they're right. I make myself laugh all the time.

Section 10
Not Feeling Good Enough

This is a really tough feeling to have. I've felt it throughout my whole life. It's prevented me from dating a lot and it's severely impacted me in making friends. I used to always feel that I was not as good as everyone else. I've come to realize that I was very wrong. We are all good enough. No one is below or above anyone. If you like someone, tell them! They are not better than you at all and you have to realize that you are perfect just the way you are. Don't change for anyone. Only change because it's what you want to do.

Unfortunately, many teenagers feel that they are above others, and that's how they act. It makes me very upset to see teenagers act like that, but there isn't much you can do to make them feel otherwise. Some people are just raised to feel that they are better than everyone else, and some learn it over time, but it's not true either way.

Many teens are very materialistic. They think that money, a new car, expensive clothes, and a huge house means that you're better than the rest of your classmates. That is not true at all. Money does not make you better than someone else. I do not like people that brag about how much money they have just to make others feel down on themselves. Whether you are a millionaire or whether you're homeless we are all still human. Don't judge others for the lifestyle they are living.

Physical looks do not make you better than someone either. Let me tell you something, if everyone thinks you're "hot", it really doesn't matter. You'll get a lot of dates in high school and everyone will think you're super popular. But when you get to real life, that isn't how it works. Most adults don't act like teenagers. Looks don't really matter. You being super "hot" won't make much of a difference if you have an awful personality. When it comes down to it what's better, someone who is extremely rude to others but is extremely attractive? Or someone who isn't a top model, but has a caring and loving personality and would do anything to make you happy? Everyone should be confident in how they look, but no one should feel the need to make others feel that they're below them. Love, kindness, and honesty is what builds a strong relationship, not your physical attractiveness. That goes for any kind of human relationship.

Don't underestimate yourself, because you're much stronger and have many more talents than you think and others will eventually see that as well. You are more than good enough and one day you will realize that. Do not ever settle for anything less than what you deserve and you deserve the very best. No matter who you are.

You're you for a reason. You may not know right now, but you'll eventually see the amazing qualities you have. I didn't understand why people liked me until I was around nineteen. Then I started understanding what other people saw in me.

When I was in high school I had terrible acne, I was overweight, I was loud and annoying, I had bad anxiety, and I was often pretty awkward in most social situations. But I was a really good kid. I was always the teen that everyone came to for advice and I was always very good at helping other people out. I would do anything to make someone else's day and that's a really good quality to have. So as I got older, I lost weight and the acne went away, but I still maintained the same personality and that's why people wanted to be around me. It still is the reason. You don't have to be popular, 'hot', or the star football player/cheerleader to have friends. Be yourself and eventually people will start seeing who you really are. Don't put on a facade and act fake as that will bring you the wrong kind of friends, ones that will use you. Not true friends.

For Parents

Children and teenagers can become insecure due to many different things. It's important to not be too tough on your teen as this can often be a cause for their insecurities. If you constantly tell them that they need to change their appearance or that their grades suck, they will start to feel that they aren't good enough for you.

Instead, show your children that you always support them and that you only want the best for them. Tell them that you know how worthy they are of love and support and that they're perfect just as they are, even if they make mistakes. Newsflash for you, ALL teenagers make mistakes. None of them are perfect

so don't think that if your child makes a mistake,
they're the only one who's ever done it. They aren't.

Section 11
A Child Of Divorce

As a child of divorce, I understand how hard it is to deal with. All the questions you have are hard to get answered. Why is this happening? Is this my fault? Am I the reason my parents are ending their relationship? These are questions almost every teenager wonders while being the child of divorced parents. Sometimes it can be hard to go to school because people may wonder why your parents aren't together anymore and your friends may not understand what's going on. It might be awkward for you to show up at sporting events or a concert and you're only with one parent.

The most important thing to remember is that it is NOT your fault. If your parents choose to get a divorce, it has nothing to do with you. You did not cause it and you are not any part of the reasoning behind it. Sometimes adults fall in love with each other and try to make it work, but sometimes it doesn't always go how we want it to go. Sometimes something happens between them that can't be worked out, but that still has nothing to do with you. I hear a lot "I think it's my fault because I was a bad kid and misbehaved a lot". Even if you were the most misbehaved child alive it still is not the reason their marriage is hurting. I know how it feels to be living in a broken home so you aren't alone. Divorce is extremely hard to get through, especially when you don't understand what's really going on.

The other day on one of my Instagram accounts my organization received a message from a sixteen year old girl who needed help getting through her situation. She was very upset that her father had abandoned her and her mom. She felt like it was her fault that he decided to leave. It's sad how many parents walk away from their kids and their homes, but it does happen. It is not your fault. Nothing you could have done could cause them to drop their life and start a new one. It's a really tough thing to go through especially when they just walk out of your life with no reason as to why they left. Kids and teenagers have a lot of pressure in their lives like in school.

Home should be a place to go to escape the stress of daily life, but unfortunately home can be where the most stress is caused. Not every child has a great home life and not every child has amazing and supportive parents so don't assume that they do. Not every kid has a great family and a stress free life. That's why I always say not to judge anyone without living their life. You have no clue what someone is going through so don't harass or bully them because you think they are an easy target. Be kind to everyone, is that so hard?

Take it one step at a time. Remember that they are both your parents. You may get mad at them because you don't understand how they could do this and it's okay to be angry. You feel as if they are breaking apart your life. I felt the same way. I didn't understand how they could do that to me. My parents got divorced during my senior year of high school and it impacted me a lot. Trying to balance school, sports, band, college preparation, a social life, and a divorce all at once is quite difficult. It takes time to work through it. Remember that your parents love you and that they aren't doing this to hurt you. You will realize that eventually, but I know it's tough at first especially if you're older and have gotten used to things being how they are over the years.

My parents taught me that love is not forever, but if it's the right person then nothing will come in between you guys which I soon came to learn. Stay strong and always trust your gut!

For Parents

You must always do what is best for your child as they need to be your main priority, even if your marriage is falling apart. It's important to plan activities for your child or teenager. Disappointing your children may have adverse effects on them as they already feel let down due to your divorce.

Parents or the families of either parent should NEVER bad talk the opposite parent and no one should manipulate the child or teenager into disliking one parent, even if that parent made bad mistakes which caused the divorce. It's important to encourage a healthy relationship with both parents as well as with both sides of the family.

Parents should always attend their teens' events, concerts, sports games, and award ceremonies. Don't do a 'one parent goes to one event and the other parent goes to the next' type of thing. It's important for the child to see **both** parents supporting them at their event or concert. Also remember, support your child and be there for them through this. It will be just as hard for them as it is for you.

Section 12
Family Abandonment

I know the feeling. A few years ago, I ended up losing a lot of my family. They just simply didn't care. They thought I hurt their "perfect family image" so they pretty much disowned me and I never heard from them again. I haven't talked to any of them in over two years. When I tried to commit suicide, they didn't visit me in the hospital, never called, never asked how I was, nothing. I will never understand what I did wrong. How do you wake up one day and one side of your family doesn't want to talk to you anymore? It honestly hurts. I still am not over it. Even though I was just a kid and didn't do anything wrong, I still always ask myself what I did to cause them to all hate me. I tried so many times to figure out why, but I never did. It really is an awful feeling and it's a hurtful feeling like you aren't good enough for your own family.

Family is supposed to always love you, protect you, and be there for you, but that isn't the case for every teenager. I can't tell you why families do this sometimes, but all I can say is that I want so much better for my future kids. I want them to grow up with a loving family, even if it's a small one. If you grew up with a loving family, lots of friends, and a great support system, then you better appreciate that because every teenager doesn't grow up with that.

You can't keep holding onto someone that won't be there for you because that will just cause tons and tons of heartbreak in the future. If you had to grow up with only one, or even no parents then I am very sorry. It's awful how parents can have a kid and just walk away like it's nothing. I don't understand how someone can just leave their own blood. It's disgusting but it happens frequently in this country. People have sex, have kids, then don't want to take any responsibility so they just leave. If you decide to have sex, then you need to be the one to step up and take responsibility of YOUR child. If you can't take care of them yourself then make sure they're safe wherever they need to be. Remember it isn't your kids' fault that you did what you did so do not give them a bad life because of the choices that you made. The child always comes first in life, no matter who you are, where you are, or what you do.

To the Family That Abandoned Me

Thank you. You made me feel like I wasn't good enough. You made me feel like I wasn't a good grandson or nephew. You made me cry myself to sleep some nights because I felt like I was alone. You made me wonder if I wasn't good enough to be a part of your family. Was it because I tried to kill myself so you felt ashamed? I was alone because of you. When something happened to me, I had no one to talk to and no one to give me advice. I had to figure it out on my own. When I'd win an award, or when my nonprofit became very successful, or when the governor reached out to me to congratulate me, you never were there. You never called. You never cared. I have done so many things with my life and you were never there for any of them. Because of you, I always thought that there was something wrong with me. I felt like I needed to improve myself so I was worthy of love and support from my own family and friends. Thank you for everything that you've taught me. I now know how great I will treat my future kids. I want them to know that their family will always be there for them no matter what.

Section 13
Family Abuse

Now, I'm not talking about the time when your mom grounded you because you failed a math test or the time that she took your phone away from you. I'm talking about abusive parents. If you're going through abuse at home, then there is one main thing to remember. It is by no means your fault. Parents abuse their kids for many different reasons, but none of them are okay. I know what it feels like to get abused and neglected by family. It's an awful feeling because family is supposed to be the place you can go home to and feel safe. Sadly though, many kids and teenagers go home to abusive, scary, and neglectful homes. The worst part is that kids are too scared to go tell someone and the outside world of people usually don't see any signs of abuse so it's hard for people to know what's going on behind closed doors. This leaves kids feeling lonely and scared which is not a way to live life.

Physical abuse is very scary, but it's not the only form of abuse. Many kids are emotionally and mentally abused while they go through childhood. You see parents get so angry at their kids for no reason and you see kids act so scared around their parents because they don't know what will happen next. Mental abuse from a parent can really destroy a child's life and can severely hurt their future.

If you are being abused at home, please call the child abuse hotline or text into the crisis hotline. People are here to help you and people are here to protect you. No child should live through abuse and no child should have to go home feeling scared of what mom and dad will do next. I know it can be extremely scary to reach out for help because you want to protect your parents and don't want them to get into trouble, but you have to protect yourself first. No one deserves abuse. No teenager deserves to go home and feel controlled by their loved ones and no teenager deserves to go home and get hit, sexually abused, or ridiculed by anyone in their home.

Not all of us have amazing home lives with amazing families and parents. Don't assume that someone has a good home life just because you do. Not all families are the same. Some teenagers blame their parents for everything. They think their parents are abusing them when all they're being is a good parent looking out for what's best for them. However, that's not always the case. Sometimes children and teens have to face horrible living circumstances because of their parents. Sometimes it's physical and sometimes it's more emotional or mental. It's honestly all just as equally scary.

A lot of times abuse is not easily stopped because we get scared and we aren't sure who to tell. Plus sometimes we assume that no one would ever abuse their own flesh and blood.

If your parents are physically or mentally abusing you, then you need to talk to someone about it. Just talking to someone can release so much stress off of you. Do not ever keep it all inside, because that will mentally destroy you. You have to get out your pain and anger before it builds up. I know we should all love our parents, but sometimes it's very hard when they treat you so horribly. It is okay to feel hatred and it's okay to cry. It's normal to feel this way.

Help yourself before it leads to depression and

anxiety. Don't put yourself through hell for people that don't care enough to treat you how you deserve to be treated.

I know what it feels like to have no support as well as going through the constant mental abuse. I hear all the time that "there's no way a parent can abuse their kid, all parents love their children". That's not always true. Like I said earlier, just because you have a good support system in your life doesn't mean everyone else does as well. With all of that being said, remember, it is never your fault. Don't forget that.

If you're being sexually abused by a family member (or by anyone), try to leave the house and contact the sex abuse hotline or call your police department. Often times with sex abuse, parents don't believe the child, especially if the child is accusing a relative. If this happens to you, try to get to a safe place and contact the police department. Talk to a trusted adult or relative. If your relatives don't believe you, either call the hotline or tell a counselor or teacher if you're still in school. You cannot pretend like it didn't happen, even if your family makes you feel that way.

Section 14
Peer Pressure

Peer pressure is one of the hardest things to have to deal with going through middle school as well as high school. Peer pressure leads to bad decisions which in some cases can follow us around for the rest of our lives. Most cases of peer pressure involve drugs, alcohol, sexual encounters, or reckless behavior. Sometimes we find ourselves in dangerous situations because we just want to fit in with our peers. Is it really ever worth it, just to fit in with a group of people?

I can tell you from experience that it's definitely not worth it. Listen, peer pressure is tough on everyone. We all want to fit in, especially during our teenage years, but some teenagers go way too far to fit in with their peers. Fitting in is not worth the consequences. Do not drink, smoke, vape, have sex, or take drugs just because other people are doing it and they're considered 'popular'.

A lot of teenagers strive to be popular in middle and high school. They do whatever it takes to be popular, including a lot of extremely stupid things. Why do teenagers want to gain so much popularity? Honestly, it's because we all simply just want to fit in. I was never easily peer pressured. I didn't really care who told me to do what. If I felt that it was wrong, I wouldn't do it, no matter what the outcome would be. I had a lot of friends who were easily persuaded by peer pressure though. I hated it. I could never understand why people would do crazy things just to make new friends.

Listen, I know you just want to fit in. I get it. I'll be honest here, most of the popular kids at school are the ones partying, drinking, staying out late, and smoking, but that doesn't mean that you need to do it as well. You don't need to be popular to matter. I wasn't popular by any means in high school and look how I turned out. Just fine. I felt just how you did. I wanted everyone to know who I was. I wanted to be the kid that everyone wanted to be friends with. The kid that everyone wanted to follow on social media. But guess what? I wasn't that kid, or anything close. It made me depressed then, but now I realize that popularity is useless. Out of all the friends I had in school, I only stayed in close contact with like two of them. To be honest, high school friendships don't mean much after school is finished. You may keep a few throughout college, but it's rare to have many, if any, past then. Don't make stupid decisions to fit in with people who aren't even going to be your real friends. Instead, do your own thing, make yourself happy, and eventually people will see the real you and will want to be your friend. It may not be the popular kids, but who cares? Be yourself because that's the best thing to do in high school, middle school, and college.

You should not be doing drugs or smoking just to fit in with the other kids in your grade. If so, then you are hanging around the wrong group of people. Drugs and alcohol are very serious things and they can lead to very severe consequences as well. What happens if you get arrested for drug possession because you just wanted to 'fit in'? Don't think it'll be too cool then.

Listen, I understand that you all want to fit in. I get that. But don't fall victim to peer pressure just because you are feeling lonely. And most importantly do not ever do something you feel uncomfortable with under any circumstances. You are in charge of your body and what you do with it. Don't let anyone else convince you into doing something you know is wrong. It won't end well. It is never worth it.

Section 15
Cheating In Relationships

This one is awful. It's happened to me so I totally understand how it feels to be cheated on. It's an extremely painful feeling, but I promise it isn't the end of the world. Don't forget that it's not your fault that they chose to do what they did. Finding out that you've been cheated on is like finding out that you've been betrayed by the person you loved most. They broke your trust. It's hard going from talking to someone all day everyday to never getting to talk to them. It's hard to erase all the memories and to have to sleep everyday knowing that you can't talk to them right when you wake up. It'll be tough for a while. You may go through a spout of sadness. That's normal with a breakup.

Try to talk to your friends and family. Lean on them for support. Do NOT go through this alone. You might feel embarrassed, but don't be. It's not your fault that they showed their true colors. They made that choice so really sit down and think about whether they deserve a second chance. Many people will give that person multiple chances which I hate seeing. The cheater is now just using them because they know if they cheat, nothing will happen so they continue to just keep doing it. That's very wrong. I'm the type of person where if you do it once, I'm done. It's extremely hard for me to trust in the first place so once you break that, I won't be able to trust you again so it's over.

If you cheated, all I have to say to you is why? They treated you so well and loved you more than themselves, yet you chose to cheat with someone else. It's disgusting and if you do it then you clearly didn't love them. People that are in love don't cheat. It's just that simple. "I'm sorry, I really do love you." Really, they love you? Makes sense. Don't let them fool you. If they loved you they wouldn't have cheated. Also, the "you didn't give me enough attention so I looked for it elsewhere" excuse is just as bad. If you feel lonely in your relationship and need more attention then talk to your partner, don't cheat. There is absolutely no good reason to cheat. None.

If they cheated, it's not your fault. I can't say that enough. They might make you feel that way, but they are just doing that to toss the blame off of themselves.

They still are the one who crossed the line, not you. If you've been cheated on, I'm really sorry. No one deserves that and it doesn't mean you aren't good enough. It means that they have an issue with themselves. Really sit down and evaluate the whole situation to decide what you should do, talk to your friends so you can get some unbiased, honest opinions about what you should do next. You can't allow someone to continuously take advantage of you. If it happens once, it's on them. If you let it keep happening to you then you need to evaluate why you're letting some trashy person bring you down.

Always remember, you deserve the best. Someone out there will love you and only you.

Section 16
Teenage Love

Love is a very strange thing. People fall in love so quickly, but fall out of love even quicker. You see people, primarily teenagers "in love" with someone then three days later "in love" with someone completely different. How is this even possible? Well, just because the word "love" is used, doesn't mean that it's a genuine feeling. So many people say "I love you" everyday but does everyone really mean it?

See, when I was young I loved everything. I loved pasta, pizza, my bike, my toy cars, and the cute girl that sat next to me in class. I mean that's just normal for kids. Kids don't know the meaning of love, at least the complex meaning of it as to do with relationships. It's usually high school where we find ourselves in our first more "serious" relationship. I'm using the word "serious" very loosely.

High school relationships are always very tough. There is a large amount of stress on a teenager as it is, and when you throw a relationship on top of it, the stress levels rise even more. A lot of the time, there's a feeling of jealousy when your significant other is around other people, and sometimes first relationships can be abusive, or full of control which is not healthy at all. In high school, at least for some kids, there is this pressure that you have to be in a relationship, like it's mandatory. No, that's very false. Some people simply don't like being in relationships, especially when there's already so much pressure with school and friends.

I'm that type of person. I don't "date" like most teenagers do. I don't want a girlfriend just to have one or just so I'm not single. That isn't real love. I don't want to be one of those people who date somebody different each month just to say they're with someone. There's no point in that. Maybe it's fun while it's happening but I'd rather focus on my life, and when the right person comes along, I'll be ready.

Falling in love with your best friend. Now, if you've been through this, you probably know how much pain this causes. Normal crushes are usually easy to get over. You like someone, it doesn't work, so you move on. But when it comes to your best friend, can you really move on? I mean they are your best friend after all. You meet someone, and you guys just click and you guys get along well together. Then you start trusting them and soon you know everything about each other, you talk everyday, and you guys have a special love for each other. It's a special feeling to have when you have a bestfriend that you truly do love. But what happens when that loves turns into something more? Tough question to answer. You talk to them all day, everyday, you know everything about them, you guys always get along, you love each other, and you guys even act like you're dating sometimes, so it's normal to get stronger feelings.

I always feel that dating relationships are great between best friends. You know each other inside and out, you know who they truly are, so it can make for a more loving, fun relationship. Most people will say they're scared to hurt the friendship if things go bad. But, in reality if they truly are your best friend, things should not go badly, and if they did, the friendship should not be ruined. The worst feeling is loving a close friend while watching them love someone else. That's a seriously painful feeling and it's one that's extremely hard to get over.

Just remember, if something feels wrong in your heart, than it probably is wrong. Don't force yourself into a relationship just to be like everyone else. You're you, and when you're ready to love someone, you will. Don't let other people pressure you, just because they are in relationships. And remember, the person that you would least expect dating might be the person that would treat you better than anyone else could.

Section 17
Going Through A Breakup

Break ups can be very hard. I haven't had many, but I still have felt the pain of a break up. Like with cheating, when you first go through a breakup, it feels like a shock, like 'how could this happen?'. You believe that it's a mistake and that your life is ruined. You may even feel like you just lost your entire world.

One day, you see them all the time, you kiss them goodnight, you fall asleep in their arms, and you do everything with them. The next day they leave you with a broken heart and a thought of how you'll ever get through this feeling of extreme loneliness. Most people get through a break up in phases: shock, denial, self doubt, anger, and acceptance. It can be hard whether you've been dating for six weeks or six years. I truly believe that time doesn't make love, chemistry and connection with another person does. Time can *build* love and a relationship, however.

When you first go through a breakup, many teens want to get revenge for getting hurt, so they take to social media. This is the worst mistake you can make here. Do not take to social media to spread info about him or her and don't create drama online because you want to get your side out there. Keep it between you guys so it can be resolved the right way. I see many immature posts on Facebook about breakups and cheating and it just makes them all look so terrible. I get that they hurt you, but don't air all their dirty laundry out on Facebook. Remember, your family, police officers, colleges, and job managers could all stumble on that type of stuff.

Instead, talk it out with loved ones. Realize that you both made mistakes and that it just wasn't meant to be. That doesn't mean you aren't good enough or that they want better. It just means that you two weren't right for each other. If it was meant to be, they'll find their way back to you. That's how love works. Don't drown yourself waiting for someone who isn't loving you how you should be loved. You have to eventually move on and focus on yourself for a while.

There are so many emotions involved in a breakup including anger, sadness, loneliness, feelings of rejection and uncertainty about the future, especially if you've been dating for a while. Particularly in the early stages of a breakup, you need to just let yourself feel whatever you're feeling. Don't hide your feelings as this will make the breakup process a lot longer and harder to deal with. Write out your thoughts in a journal or talk to a friend about them so you don't feel alone.

Section 18
Letting Go Of People

I have a problem with letting go of people, especially if I know it'll be good for me. I struggle to say goodbye to people that leave my life, even when I deserve better than most of them (I know that sounds bad). It's a lot harder than it seems and you'll realize this once you have to go through it. I have been hurt a lot by family members, friends, and strangers, but I can never find a way to let them go. I tell myself that they don't deserve me and that I don't need the stress in my life, but then I find myself answering their calls or texts if they need me for help. I'm notorious for letting people hurt me and then taking them back when they're lonely or need help. I honestly think that's what causes my trust issues. I open myself up to people and they just take it and chew it up and spit it out and move on like they never even gave a shit about how I felt.

I have had people claim that they loved me and would never leave and yet one day they walked out of my life like I meant nothing to them. I tried not blaming myself, but it's hard. I thought it was my fault, but after a while, you start not caring what people think of you. It really isn't your fault if people leave your life (unless you actually did something wrong or illegal). Most people just do it because they want something new or are sick of relationships/friendships. Lots of teenagers use this shitty excuse, but it's whatever. Don't pay any attention to it. Keep your real friends and your family close. Don't dump your true friends for new ones who show you attention. That will always turn around to bite you.

If you are trying to part ways with someone then here is some tips on how you can say goodbye:
1. You will feel heartbroken and that is totally okay. It's normal, because if you have been close to someone for so long but then have to say goodbye to them, it can be extremely hard. No one is expecting you to get over it in two days. Take as much time as you need because we all move on in different ways and we all take different lengths of time to move on from someone we love. Whether it be a relationship or just a friendship. Realize that you deserve

better and they just simply can't give you that.
2. Make sure you know why you had to say goodbye. If you're letting go of someone close to you, then there's obviously a good reason. Don't second guess yourself and remember that you did it for the best.
3. You will miss them like crazy and that's normal. Don't feel obligated to take them back because you miss them. If you take them back then you might be setting yourself up for another heartbroken goodbye.
4. Make new friends or eventually find a new person to fall in love with. Depending on the person, it might take a while for this to happen and that's okay. Take your time! But, remember not everyone is like them, so don't treat the new people you meet like the person you said goodbye to. Everyone won't treat you the same.
5. When you're ready, get rid of all reminders of your past relationship or friendship if you choose to. When you

know it's for certain over, let go. Delete text messages and get rid of things that make you remember them. It's really hard to do and not everyone does it. If you feel you have to do it, then do it. It'll help you move on if you don't see daily reminders of them and your relationship.

Remember that you are still amazing and you're very strong for letting go. It's very hard to do so don't worry if you really struggle to let go of someone, I still do...

Section 19
Losing Someone Due To Suicide

It is not your fault. This is most important when going through something like this. Here's something almost no one knows about me. When I was sixteen my best friend had committed suicide and I was one of the last people she had talked to. For months I felt guilty like I should have stopped her, like I should have been there for her that night. But in all reality she didn't give any signs that she would take her life. Unfortunately there really was no way of knowing what would happen. I wish I was trained in suicide prevention back then so I could have recognized her pain and helped her. I wish I could have held her hand and told her that everything was going to be okay.

I still miss her to this day. If you lost a friend either by suicide or something else then I am truly sorry. I know how it feels and it is very hard to have to live with it. There's always a little feeling of being guilty like you should have stopped them, but trust me, it's not your fault. Suicide is hard to understand. Why would she do that? Why would it happen? As someone who's tried to commit suicide, I don't even understand it myself sometimes. Please, if you're struggling reach out for help. I didn't deal with my best friend passing away very easily. If someone close to you passes away, it's hell to have to deal with. Don't deal with it alone. Please.

It's okay to wonder why they would do that to themselves and to their family and it's even okay to be angry. While it isn't your fault, blaming yourself is natural as is wondering why they'd do this. The question will always be there. "Didn't she care about me?" "Why would she do this to me?" Those questions are normal to ask yourself at the beginning. Suicide leaves a lot of questions and unfortunately they usually cannot be answered. Just remember that they didn't want to hurt you. It isn't their fault or yours. They loved you, even if you don't see that right now.

Section 20
Advice For Every Teenager

You're perfect just the way you are. I'm tired of seeing girls (and boys) change the way they look and act just because their partner said to. If you have a boyfriend, he better treat you the way you deserve to be treated. And if he tries to change the person you are, then he isn't the one for you.

If you like music, listen to it. If you like reading, find a great book. If you like soccer, become the star player. Don't let any guy or girl dictate what you can do and where you can go. I see so many girls getting controlled by their boyfriends and it isn't right. Date someone who loves you the way you are. Someone who loves all of your flaws and insecurities. You want someone to like you the way you are, not because they changed you to what they wanted you to be.

Sometimes we get ourselves into relationships that are hard to get out of, you feel so attached to them, and you feel like if you weren't dating them, your life would
end. Trust me, I've been through this, but the truth is it won't end, because you're much stronger than this. It will be tough to move on, but you have to realize that you're worth more than how he or she is treating you.

Think about this. It's going to feel awful when you have to end the relationship, BUT how will you feel when you have someone who treats you right, doesn't cheat on you, and truly loves you? Amazing right? So why are you with him if all he does is bring you down? I hate to say it, but if he really loved you, he wouldn't cheat, abuse you, or purposely make you upset. Real men (and women) would never hurt the person they're with. So to every single teenager out there, remember this. Letting go is hard, but sometimes it is a necessity to live a safe and happy life.

You're perfect the way you are so don't change. Be in a safe and caring relationship with someone that only loves you. And remember if you are being abused and can't find a way out, call the abuse hotline or your local police non-emergency number for help. People will help you and then you will be able to move on and be happy. We all deserve love and we all deserve to be treated with respect, so just make sure you're with the person that does that. And if you are with an abusive boyfriend or girlfriend then maybe you need to second guess your relationship.

The saddest thing to see is an amazing girl getting abused by her boyfriend because she feels that's all she deserves. No one deserves abuse. You deserve love just like everyone else. We all make mistakes, it's what makes us human. Don't let your mistakes define you. Learn from them, grow from them, and most importantly learn to love yourself. It's hard, trust me I know. But remember, you were perfect before he came into your life and made you feel that way. Do not let a guy dictate your happiness. Only you get to be in control of that. No teenager is worth going through abuse for and remember not all guys are the same. Some of us out there only care about the wellbeing of others and would never let a girl get hurt. I'm one of those people. There's nothing I hate more than seeing a guy abuse his girlfriend. Just keep all of this in mind the next time you date someone. And remember "Don't change so people will like you, be yourself and the right people will love the real you". You're perfect just the way you are. Don't forget that.

Section 21
Long Distance Relationships

Let's be real here. They suck. Sometimes they're totally worth it and you can end up meeting the person you spend your life with, but other times they can be a huge emotional burden, especially if you don't do well without physical contact. My best friend was involved in a long distance relationship for over two years. He lived fourteen hours away from her and they dated for two years, but never actually met. I personally could never do something like that, because I would always want to know what it's like to be around them. They talked everyday for two years and even fell asleep on the phone together most nights. I never really thought that love existed in the online world, but maybe it actually does. I have seen many couples meet online and have a long distance relationship and end up meeting and falling completely in love.

It can be very difficult, because most parents won't understand or allow it, especially if you're a teenager. My mom would have killed me if I ever met a girl online that was across the country when I was younger. It can also be very dangerous, because there is a lot of bad people online who use the online community as a way to lure teenagers in.

Most teenagers don't really know how to deal with long distance relationships, because there is always a lack of communication, and when you aren't together in the same city, it can be very hard to fix that problem. Teens involved in long distance relationships often can't find the trust needed to continue the relationship. This leads to accusations of cheating, lying, and manipulation. Some teenagers also believe that they'll never get caught, so they do things to break the trust of their partner. If you're in a long distance relationship, you have to have full trust of your partner, or I can promise you that it will never last. Long distance relationships are all about trust.

NEVER meet up with a person you met online if you haven't called them and video chatted with them on multiple occasions. You don't know the person until you meet them, so never go out with them alone until you actually come to realize who they really are. You never know who you meet online, so don't take the chance and do something stupid that you'll later regret. You and your boyfriend/girlfriend will want to see each other, but if you met online, maybe through a social networking site, that person may not be who they say they are. Make sure you verify who that person is before you start any kind of relationship. Don't believe everything they say, because it may not always be true.

Communication is huge for anyone involved in a long distance relationship. When you're in one, it's easy to just hang up the phone and not deal with your problems. If you're together in person, you can't do that as much. This often causes a lot of stress for the relationship, because one person may ignore the other, turn their phone off, or not want to deal with the problems of the relationship. Many long distance relationships end because of a lack of communication.

If you don't communicate about your problems, your relationship will start to crumble.

Section 22
Parents Wont Let You Date

Ah, this is by far one of the toughest pieces of advice to give. Most parents have the best intentions for you. If they tell you not to date, it's most likely because they know you well enough to know that you aren't ready for something that serious yet. In some instances, they may even see how awful your boyfriend/girlfriend is before you ever will.

Don't date until you're ready and when you are ready, make sure you date someone in your age range. If you're sixteen years old you should not be dating or even talking to twenty-five year olds. People will disagree with me on this, but I'm only looking out for you. The guy that's five years older than you when you're sixteen doesn't love you. He may say it, but no twenty-one year old should be loving a child. It's wrong and shouldn't happen. My personal advice to all the teenage girls out there is to not date someone more than a couple years (no more than two) older than you. Your parents probably won't like it and they have the right not to. I wouldn't either if I was them.

Dating is a scary place and your parents only want to protect you the best they can. So when your parents make rules about social media and dating, trust them. They usually know what they're doing. You know, I wasn't allowed to date or have social media when I was younger. I would get very mad at them and I would argue for social media all the time. My mom was always against it. She was right, in a way. Now I'm on social media and all that's on there is drama, fighting, and cyberbullying. There is absolutely no reason a child (under fourteen) should have a Facebook let alone a phone. They're children, let them be that. They should not have a phone and they should not have to date when they're really young. It all depends on maturity. If they are responsible at fifteen then fine, if they aren't responsible until they're eighteen then that's fine too.

I will be honest though. Most parents are just trying to protect their children from harm, but some go so far overboard that it becomes just as dangerous as what they're trying to prevent. Many parents (like mine) don't allow their kids to date anyone at all and I don't necessarily agree with that. I know there's a lot of bad out there, but how will you ever learn lessons and make mistakes if you can't live your life? I am NOT saying to jump up and date every person you think is attractive, but if you like someone and they like you, why not give it a shot? Instead of protecting your children, it can actually make it worse. Because my parents didn't let me date or have social media, I'd still go on social media and go crazy because I wanted attention and when I finally met a girl I liked, I had no idea what to do, because my parents always kept me away from it.

For Parents

My honest advice to parents is to not let your kids date under the age of fifteen or sixteen. After that, I believe that it depends on your child's maturity level. If they are mature and meet a good partner, let them date and see how it goes. Ask them how it's going, make sure they're safe, and set boundaries for what the couple can do, where they can go, and when they need to be home. If they aren't mature, talk to them about it. Explain to them that you just don't feel comfortable with them dating. Keep in mind that they are a teenager and will most likely still go behind your back. It's wrong and I advise against it, but if a teen wants to date, they will, whether you like it or not.

Don't force your child to break up with someone they're dating (unless abuse is occuring), because your child will begin pushing you away, especially if they truly love the person they're dating. Most parents say that teens don't know what love is yet and that we're all stupid and don't know how to handle a relationship. I disagree. Just because we're young adults or teens doesn't mean we're clueless. I have seen some parents alienate their child for who they chose to date and they end up hating their child's partner for very small or in reality, stupid reasons. My advice to all parents is to talk to your child, give their boyfriend/girlfriend a chance, and respect them. Maybe they're in a really great relationship.

Many parents fail to see the significance of thinking through what they really want for their kids when it comes to dating and when they begin dating, parents have to make very quick decisions under pressure. This typically doesn't end very well.

If your child is under fifteen they should not be dating or going on a date of any kind. If your child is fifteen then I would let them date in a group setting, on a double date, with other friends, or under supervision. If your teen is between sixteen and eighteen, I'd let them date as long as they're mature, safe, and responsible enough to date someone. Make sure they know all about the risks of dating, online dating, sex, pregnancy, and dating abuse.

Section 23
Falling In Love

Someone finally comes into your life. Someone truly amazing that you know won't ever go anywhere. You guys become best friends and are very close now, closer than you are with anyone else. Now you start falling in love with them and you don't know what to do. I always advise everyone to tell them (unless it will really damage the friendship) because it's always best to just get it out there then have to keep those feelings inside. Even if they flat out reject you, at least now you won't have to keep living with the possibility of what if. If you really fell in love with them and you told them, good for you! I'm proud of you because that takes a lot of courage.

Now, what happens if they say they don't love you in that way or what if they are already dating someone? Tricky question because in reality what can you really do? Not much. It's a really crappy feeling but it's something we all have to go through, sadly. Just because they don't want to date you too doesn't mean you're not good enough. They just don't see you in that light. Dating in high school can be weird and frustrating. I've seen a girl date the worst of guys and continue to do so, but reject any good guy that comes along. It doesn't make sense, but it happens a lot. A lot of times in high school, people want to date the popular bad boy, or the popular stuck up girl. Then when they end up getting hurt, they for some reason continue to date those type of people and continuously get hurt. When a good person comes along, they typically put them in the friendzone because they don't want to lose them. It's frustrating, especially if you're the good person that just wants to treat someone right.

NEVER get in between someone's relationship, even if you like one of the people in it. That will cause a lot of issues for many people, including you. Just wait. I always say if it's meant to be, it will be. Trust me.

Just remember that if they don't have feelings for you, it doesn't mean that they don't still love you as a friend or as a person. It also does not mean that you aren't good enough for them. It just means that they have their heart set on someone else. They might not know how perfect you actually would treat them. Like I always say, love is very weird. So don't lose hope, we always end up with the one least expected.

Section 24
Pressure To Send Nude Pictures

Don't. I am not sure how to say it any differently. I understand that you're a teenager. You want to impress the boy you like and when he asks for pictures, you don't want to disappoint him so you send them. First of all, no real guy or boyfriend would pressure you or even ask you to send nude pictures to him. If he respected you and your body, he wouldn't ask.

Once you send pictures, they are now in someone else's hands. That can really destroy your life very quickly. What if he's not really who you think he is and he shows his friends or posts them online? Keep your pictures to yourself. If he pressures you then he probably isn't the right guy for you. No one should pressure someone to do something so intimate with their body,

According to TIME, 73% of teenagers today have a smartphone, giving them access to all types of communication over text or social media. The majority of teenagers don't report sexting due to feelings of embarrassment, but 15% of teens say they send sexts and 27% say they receive them.

In most places it's against the law to even send nude pictures to anyone as it's considered distributing child pornography. If you want the pictures and accept them, it can be considered possession of child pornography. I know you think that it'll never happen to you. That you'll never get caught or that the other person will never do anything with them, but what if you're wrong? What if he dumps you and spreads them around school? What if the guy you're trying to impress really isn't the guy you think he is?

Parents should not react harshly to their teens sending or receiving nude pictures (makes them hide it from you and go behind your back in the future), but should rather teach them in advance the consequences of sending or receiving nude pictures. Teach and talk to your teen about the possible legal consequences of sending or receiving nudes and how the pictures could potentially be spread around school or online. If none of this works, it may be time to take their phone away, even if they're an older teenager (fifteen to seventeen). If they're under fifteen, I advise against getting your child a phone in the first place. Children can't be responsible enough to have connections to millions of people online, including with predators.

For Teens

- The safest way to avoid a picture getting into the wrong hands is to never take it or share it.
- Never send nude pictures to your boyfriend or girlfriend. I know it seems like it's okay since you're dating, but remember, what happens if you guys break up?
- Sometimes, teens break up and one teen sends the nudes pictures out of their ex to embarrass them (sometimes called "revenge porn").
- Never take and send an image of yourself under pressure, even from someone you care about. If you feel pressure to send nudes, the person pressuring you most likely isn't treating you how you deserve to be treated. Dating is NOT about nudes and sex.
- If a stranger asks you to take nude pictures, they could be trying to set you up. NEVER send pictures of yourself even clothed to people you don't know.

- If a nude photo gets sent to your phone, first, do not send it to anyone else (could be considered distribution of child pornography). Delete the photo immediately AFTER telling your parents or a trusted adult. If they sent it to you and you don't know who they are, it may be worth checking in with the police as they may be trying to sexually abuse you or even kidnap you .
- If the picture is from a friend or someone you know, then you need to make them aware of possible consequences including child pornagraphy charges, getting the police involved, and a lot of embarrassment.

Section 25
Abusive Teenage Relationships

Hey, you finally are dating the guy or girl you have had a crush on forever, great news! Things are going so well, but then all of the sudden they change. The love you thought they had for you suddenly turns into anger. The person you felt safe with now makes you shake in fear.

Physical abuse is extremely wrong and should never happen under any circumstances. If he (or she) puts his hands on you then we need to come up with a safety plan to get you out of there. I wouldn't want to see you get hurt or see him (or her) get worse as time goes by. Emotional abuse can be just as bad, however. If he truly loves you then he wouldn't hurt you, or control you, or treat you like you don't deserve him. Sometimes teenagers get insecure and control their partner as a way to deal with their own insecurities. Or maybe they were hurt in the past so they take it out on you. That's not okay. It also is not just guys. Girls can be abusers and often times go under the radar because many people (even police

officers, judges, and lawyers) don't believe girls can abuse guys. It's quite sad actually.
No always means no and crossing that line is not okay. If he's pressuring you into sex or sexual contact then that is abuse. If he asks you and you aren't comfortable, say no. If he loves you then he will accept it and be okay. If he starts controlling you and pressuring you then that is not okay under any circumstances. You have to stand up for yourself and say no. You don't have to do whatever he wants just because you're his girlfriend. There's still boundaries that should not ever be crossed by a male or a female.

Really think about what you need to do. You aren't safe and he or she will get worse. As many times as he says he loves you and that he'll change, it's just simply not true. You can't keep putting yourself through that trauma and abuse. It isn't fair to you and if you have kids then it isn't fair to them either. I know it's hard to leave. I really do understand, but your safety needs to come first. Not what he wants. Reach out for help and maybe call the domestic violence hotline if things turn physical. Maybe call the police if you need to as they will always be there to help you stay safe from him. No one deserves abuse and you can do so much better than that. Leave him and go get what you deserve.

If you abuse a girl, what exactly is wrong with you? You think it's okay to hit, control, and lie to your girlfriend who's been there for you through everything? You cheated on her, she stayed. You hit her, she stayed. You made her lose her friends, she stayed. You controlled her life, she still stayed. And yet you still have the nerve to turn around and slap her and tell her what to do? You are truly awful and you need to get help from someone as soon as possible so you can get better. Then maybe your girlfriend won't have to live in fear every time you walk in the door.

Relationship abuse is absolutely nothing to joke about or laugh about. It's a very serious topic that needs to be talked about. I have experienced and witnessed abuse in a relationship first hand and I know the outcome it could have on someone.

I see so many abusive relationships on a daily basis and I always wonder why that person would put themselves through that. I never really understood the reasoning behind it. I know you "love him and can't leave" and I really do understand that. But why are you putting yourself through abuse just to be with someone who clearly doesn't care. If they abuse you, especially physically, then you have to make the choice of what's more important. Him or your safety. Unfortunately, often times that choice will be him.

I believe self esteem has a huge part in relationship abuse. I think sometimes the person getting abused feels that he's the most she deserves and that she doesn't deserve to be treated correctly. I also feel that the person who is doing the abuse is self conscious as well. It might explain why they take their anger out on you. It is absolutely never okay to put your hands on someone else, no matter who you are. If you can't stop abusing her, then leave. Don't put her through that because she doesn't deserve it. Physical abuse is awful but it's not necessarily always the worst.

Emotional abuse can be awful to have to experience. She might force you into things you aren't comfortable with but you do them anyways because you "love her". He might take his anger out on you, yell at you, and belittle you. Maybe even harass or bully you. That is also never okay. Verbal harassment can sometimes be more traumatizing than physical abuse. Just because he doesn't put his hands on you doesn't mean it isn't abuse. I hear that a lot actually. "Well he doesn't hit me, so it's not abuse." That is very incorrect. There are many, many, many types of abuse. And none of them are even slightly okay. Also, if they force you or persuade you to do something that you aren't comfortable with like sex or drinking then that is not okay either. You are your own body and only you control what goes on with it. Don't let him control you. He is not your boss and he does not have the right to tell you what to do. He should be supportive of you, he should appreciate you, and most importantly he should love you for who you are and not for someone you aren't. Don't ever change because a guy told you to. Change because you want to. You are perfect and beautiful just the way you are so don't let a guy make you feel otherwise. If he starts controlling you then maybe it's time to say goodbye.

I do want to talk about this because it is important. The abuser may not always be a "him". A lot of us think that abuse is always done by a guy and that is simply not true. Trust me, I know, I've been through it. The same thing goes for guys. Don't feel scared to talk to someone about it. Just because you are a guy getting abused doesn't mean it's your fault or that you are any less of a man. Based on statistics, most of the time the abuser is a male, but it doesn't mean that it can't be a girl. If you need help, please reach out!

Teen Dating Abuse Warning Signs

- Your partner demands that you run things by them before doing them (controls you and the decisions you make)
- Your partner threatens you or threatens to cause physical harm to you
- Checking your cell phone or email without permission
- Demanding that you give them the passwords to your social media accounts so that they can log on
- Constantly putting you down and/or calling you names
- Using their jealousy to control you
- Explosive temper (throwing things, punching walls, yelling and demeaning you)
- Pressuring or forcing you to have sex (includes manipulating you into sexual contact)
- Physically hurting you in any way (includes hitting, punching, slapping, spitting on you, and kicking)

- Only allowed to hang out and talk to your partner (When teens date, it's very common for them to spend all of their time together and on the phone and that's okay as they're typically just very attached to each other, but if it becomes forced by one partner, then it becomes an issue)
- Mood swings

To all you guys abusing your girlfriend, you like making her feel scared? You like making your kids worry about what you might do to their mother? Grow up, or leave her and let her be happy.

To all you girls getting abused, would you let your future daughter go through the same thing he's currently doing to you?

National Domestic Violence Hotline
1-800-799-7233
https://www.thehotline.org/

National Dating Abuse Intervention Team
1-844-767-4722 Ext #1
www.nationalyouthiscbtaskforce.org

Section 26
Sexual Abuse

It's extremely difficult to deal with sexual abuse and it's even more difficult to understand. It isn't your fault that it has happened to you. You didn't ask for it. It's tough growing up having to live with that especially when you were so young and had zero control over what was taking place.

If you were sexually abused as a child and are still struggling with it then maybe it's time to start thinking about trying to find a good counselor so you can face it and hopefully start to move on. You won't ever forget about it, but you can move on and put it past you. Remember that you were young so you didn't have any control over being able to stop it. And even if you were older and were assaulted, it still isn't your fault. None of it is.

If you were just sexually assaulted then you need to get help immediately. Call the police or the hospital and get advice on what to do next if you feel scared. Remember, if your boyfriend or girlfriend took advantage of you when you said no then that is still considered sexual assault or rape. Never give in to someone's wishes if you are not one hundred percent okay with what is going to happen. If you want to have sex and then feel you want to stop then say "stop" and that you don't want to continue. It's your body and only you get to decide what you do with it. If they continue, then they're automatically committing a crime. You have to tell a trusted adult. I know you may feel embarrassed or scared to tell someone what happened but you have to. You have to reach out for help. Do NOT keep it all inside and try to deal with it yourself. Let yourself get help.

I know it's very scary, but calling the police or going to the hospital is always the best thing to do, especially right after it happens.

If you're a parent and your child comes to you about being sexually abused, ALWAYS believe them, even if they have a history of lying. As a parent, you have the obligation to protect your child first. Even if they come to you and say that your husband/wife, boyfriend/girlfriend, sister/brother, or another relative sexually abused them, you have to believe them. Ignoring your child is the worst thing you could do in a situation like this. This shows that you don't care about them, believe them, or want to help them. Your children come first and you have to always respect that. Choosing a family member over your child gives them the impression that you don't care which will cause them to not come to you regarding important issues they're facing.

<u>One in nine girls and one in fifty-three boys under the age of eighteen experience sexual abuse or assault at the hands of an adult.</u>

<u>Females ages sixteen to nineteen are four times more likely than the general population to be victims of rape, attempted rape, or sexual assault.</u>

Rape, Abuse & Incest National Network
1-800-656-4673
https://www.rainn.org/

Section 27
Struggling With Parents

I totally understand this one. Most parents have our backs, support us, and allow us to make our own choices as we grow older, but this isn't always the case. Some parents do in fact try to control our lives, even as we graduate and are ready to grow up. Some parents are just trying to be overprotective (which is totally understandable), but some do it as a form of abuse.

Sometimes you have to stand up for yourself and make your own life decisions. Now I'm not saying you should stand up to your parents and go dropout of high school, start drinking, and go to a dozen parties, but if your parents are forcing you to attend a college you don't want to go to, then stand up to them. Another way teenagers often feel controlled by their parents is with dating. Often times, parents can see that you are dating a bad person because they are not in love, they're just trying to protect you. However, some parents try to control their child into not dating someone that's good for them. It sounds very strange, but it happens. Some parents try to keep a level of control over you and don't want anyone making you happy, because it then means that you are growing up and some parents fear that. I look at it this way, if you're being safe, smart, and are making good decisions, then stick with your gut. Don't ignore your parents' concerns though because oftentimes they do see things in your boyfriend/girlfriend that you don't see. Take a step back and just analyze your relationship. See if they have any truth to what they're saying. If not, talk to them. Don't get mad and freak out. Talk to them and see why they're concerned. Maybe they are just worried about you.

With that being said, it's your life. If you're making good and safe choices that will make you happy, then you shouldn't let anyone control your future. When you're going through high school and college, it's okay to make mistakes. It's how you learn how to handle situations. If you're making good choices, then your parents and family should support you. If it turns out to be a bad choice, then pick yourself back up and learn your lesson. Parents, NEVER say 'I told you so' to your child. It sounds innocent because you may have been right, but this will only push your child away. They'll now think that everytime they make a mistake, you'll say this, so they'll start to go behind your back. Sit down and in a calm manner, discuss the issue with your child. Show your concerns, but let them know that you are always there for them and that they need to always be safe.

For Parents

Parent your child, but also let them spread their wings a little bit. It's okay to be overprotective, but if you protect them too much, they'll never spread their wings and grow up. Then when they get thrown into adult situations, they'll have no clue what to do because you held them back for so long.

Let your teenager experience love, heartbreak, pain, failure, mistakes, learning new things, and growing up. Don't shield them too much or you may regret that when it's time for them to grow up and they don't know what to do.

Section 28
Social Media And Addictions

Social media is a great way to communicate with friends, make friends, and in some cases even meet future dating partners. It's also a place for useless drama, crime, cyberbullying, relationship abuse, and stalking. I'm sure you've heard this, but a lot of people say things online that they would never say in real life. It happens a lot actually.

Many dating relationships start online. Some start on Facebook or apps similar to it while others start on more of a dating type website like Tinder. It can be a great thing that leads to a great relationship, but it can also be dangerous.

Don't ever give your address or anything like that to a random stranger online. Seems like it's common sense, but many teenagers still do it. "Oh my god he/she is really into me, I'm going to go see them!" Bad idea. Don't go over to their house to "chill". If you want to meet an online friend, that's fine, but do it in a populated public place. That way if the fifteen year old boy turns out to be a fifty year old man, you'll be in public so nothing will happen to you. I am not joking with the last statement either. You'd be surprised at how many adults pose as teenagers online just so they can meet up with them. There's a lot of people like this online so be careful. Don't trust someone just because they say that they are who they really are. How do you really know?

I'm going to get hate for saying this, but no thirteen year old girl should be talking to strangers online. Many parents don't have an issue with it which seems very wrong to me, but oh well. I do agree that parents should let their kids have freedom to a certain limit on their phones. But that means that you, the child, have to be responsible. Do you think your parents want to get a visit from the police department telling them that you are missing because you wanted to meet the guy you were talking to online and he turned out not to be what you thought he would be? Happens a lot, so be careful. Social media is a great thing for millions of people, but it only takes one bad person to get on there and hurt a child. Just be smart with who you talk to.

I hate seeing useless drama on social media. People posting stupid things and then tagging the person it's about just to bring attention to the fight. Let me break it to you, no one cares. You had a fight with your best friend so you think you're a real tough, cool person for posting the text screenshots and tagging the person to "embarrass them". Again, I hate to break it to you, but it doesn't make you look cool. It makes you look quite stupid actually. I see these statuses about fights and drama all the time. Usually they have hundreds of comments because all these random people come in and take sides and encourage the childish behavior.

My favorite is when someone posts "100 likes and I'll post the video of the fight I was in". Seriously? I only have to say one thing to everyone who posts all this drama on Facebook, grow up. College is coming. Your future is coming. Remember, you never know who will see your drama and the bullying that you post. Colleges and future employers might stumble upon it. That would be awful, wouldn't it? You may not care now, but you will one day. Hopefully you don't learn the hard way.

I used to be addicted to social media. I would post fifteen statuses a day and I was honestly just looking for attention. I look back today and I'm honestly embarrassed at the things I used to post. It was quite clear that I was just searching for attention so I could validate that people actually did like me. I didn't have social media till I was around sixteen or seventeen and I created it without my mom knowing. She never allowed me to have a phone or be on any sort of social media, so I didn't even know what social media was when I was younger. The other kids used to pick on me for that as well and they'd always laugh at me because I didn't have a Facebook or Snapchat account.

When I finally created Facebook, Instagram, and Snapchat accounts, I sort of went crazy with it. It was like an instant connection to all of these people and I went completely overboard. I'd friend random people just so I'd have lots of Facebook friends and I'd post statuses just because I wanted a lot of likes so I'd feel important. If I didn't get a lot of likes I'd feel depressed and lonely.

Based on experience, I can honestly tell you, don't do it. Don't look for attention online, it makes you look really desperate and you'll regret it when you're older. I hate to break it to you, but the amount of Instagram followers you have and the amount of Snapchat streaks you hold is completely and utterly useless. I see lots of teenagers completely addicted to Snapchat to the point where it's worrisome to watch. If you're sending thousands of snaps a day just to keep up streaks with random people you don't know, I think there may be a problem. Why would you send pictures of yourself to keep a streak with some random person who added you online? That's extremely scary to me, especially since a lot of teenagers keep their location on in some social media apps. Maybe it's just me, but there's something very frightening about random strangers on my Snapchat seeing exactly where I'm located at any given time as they send fifty streaks a day to me. Maybe that's just me though.

You don't need to be addicted to social media to feel wanted. Most people you meet online aren't true friends to begin with. A large amount of teens you meet online want nudes, sex, are older than they claim, or are not exactly who they appear to me. During my time running the organization, I've met hundreds of teenage girls who were addicted to social media because they were desperate for attention from guys so they would feel wanted and like they're pretty enough. That is not the way to get attention, as it's actually quite dangerous. It's okay to admit that you have low self esteem and an attention problem. I did. You have to because you can't let your attention seeking problem online continue, because if it does, it could turn into a very dangerous situation if you meet the wrong person.

Section 29
Bullying

Bullying is something that is very serious but is rarely taken seriously. It's very unfortunate that some teenagers feel the need to bully others. It's not necessary and frankly it's quite disgusting. I was bullied some in school for many different things and it does hurt. It causes depression, anxiety, eating disorders, self harm, and sometimes even suicide.

Words hurt. Sometimes even more than physical bullying. Bullying can include name calling, hitting, fighting, making fun of someone for who they are, or even harassment, or stalking. The most common type of bullying is cyberbullying because teens feel that they can say whatever they want online and feel they have no consequences. I knew a young girl who committed suicide because of bullying and it's very tragic. She was a great girl who had such a bright future ahead of her. The worst part is that it doesn't need to happen. There is absolutely no reason to bully someone. I've seen people get bullied for being different, autistic, gay, overweight, depressed, having an eating disorder, for self harming, and so much more and it's all disgusting.

What gives you even the slightest of rights to take time out of your day to make someone else feel like shit? I was mainly bullied because I used to cut. My parents would yell at me because they didn't understand and my friends and school classmates would laugh at me because they didn't understand how serious it was. At one point, no one really understood what was going on with me and why I was cutting. I used to wear hoodies everyday to school and kids would pull my sleeves up just to make jokes or ask me why I'd be so 'stupid' to do something like that. Let me tell you, it hurts. It's hard to hear. There was no reason as to why I had to be treated like that, but I was. That's bullying.

If your friend is cutting their skin, they're obviously struggling enough so you don't need to cause them to harm themselves more. If they have a different sexaul preferance than you, so what? I'm not gay so I can't relate to this one, however it's 2018/2019 people. Either accept them or ignore them. They have an eating disorder. So? Why does that affect you? Eating disorders are hard enough to go through without your harassment and degradement. It's as simple as that. If you don't like what someone is doing or who they are then maybe try and help them instead of tormenting them. There is no need to pick on them or make them feel bad. You think they are "weird"? Well who made you perfect? Who gave you the right to decide who's weird or different? We are all different. It's what makes us, us. Just because you think you're popular doesn't mean you can bully anyone you think is below you. Newsflash for you, no one is below you.

Now, let's talk about this cyberbullying garbage. Seriously? You need to sit behind a screen and make fun of people because you're too insecure with your own self? Cyberbullying usually (not always) is targeted more towards females. I constantly see statuses on Facebook making fun of the appearance of how some girl's look, or what she decided to wear to school, or what she likes to do in her free time. So this person looks a certain way so you decide to make statuses about her, bad talk her to her friends, harass her, and then bully her? All over a girl you don't even know? Seems pretty disgusting to me, right? If you are insecure with your own body or self, do NOT take that out on innocent people. It's not their fault that you do not like yourself or feel insecure. I understand if you have low self esteem, as do I, but that cannot be an excuse to bully. It's not okay. They don't know you and you don't know them. Don't pick on someone that has self esteem issues just to make yourself feel better. That's truly awful and it happens so much and it needs to stop, now. Grow up.

If you are getting bullied and can't stand up for yourself then please get help. You do not deserve what you are going through and it needs to stop. Go tell a teacher or a family member as soon as it starts happening. All too many times bullying between teens has led to suicide or in some cases even homicide. I've seen many cases in which a teenager was getting bullied and they could no longer handle it so they decided to take their own life to end all of the pain and harassment. And in some rare cases, someone may try to get revenge on their bully because they can no longer handle it and that can lead to fighting, suspension, and sometimes something worse. So let's say the kid in school that you're bullying doesn't show up to school one day and you feel sad because you have nobody to pick on today. You have a school assembly and find out that the kid you're bullying has committed suicide because of what you did. Could you handle being the reason they committed suicide?

"#endbullying"

It was my first day at Greenfield High School. I was forced to move from my home town because my dad switched jobs hoping to bring home some more money. It seemed like a nice city and a nice community of people. My old school was very small and it was the kind of town where everyone knew everyone. If you walked into the grocery store, you'd end up knowing everyone in there. I did miss my old school and my friends but I was a little excited to start fresh and meet new people.

I woke up extra early to make sure I had all of my stuff together, and I wanted to look as good as I could look for all the new people I'd meet. I wanted my first day of high school to be as good as it possibly could be. My mom and I got in the car and we headed to school and I started feeling butterflies in my stomach. I didn't know what to expect when I got to my new school. We eventually arrived and I got out of the car and took a deep breath and walked toward the door. I said bye to my baby sister as I entered the building. She looked up to me like a role model. I've always loved her so much. Most siblings always fight and argue but that wasn't like us. She always came to me for advice and she always put me before anyone else in her life.

I opened the door to the school and stepped inside. I closed my eyes and took a long, deep breath of fresh air to calm my nerves down.

I went to the main office first because we all had to pick up our schedules. I walked through many groups of people to get there. It was a pretty long walk and my asthma started, kicking in after smelling cigarettes coming from the bathrooms. I finally made it to the office and as I went to open the door, it flung open and some kid came charging out of there cursing and screaming. Apparently someone wasn't having a good first day at school. I slowly walked over to the lady at the desk. I picked up my schedule and headed toward the door. I walked down the hallway trying to read my class list while trying to manage walking straight down the hallway. It's my first day of school and I didn't want to embarrass myself by falling or tripping in the hallway...

That didn't work out so well as I ran into someone and dropped my schedule so I bent over and picked it up. As I stood back up, I couldn't believe what was in front of me. The prettiest girl I have ever seen. Her eyes sparkled, her hair shined, and her smile was pulling my heart right out of my chest. She looked at me and said "hi I'm Lauren, are you new here?" I said "yes I just moved here, today is my first day, I'm Paul." She smiled and asked if I wanted to walk her down the hallway to her first class. Of course the answer was yes. We walked for about three minutes before reaching the door of her first class. We got to know each other a little bit and we exchanged phone numbers before she walked away. Seems kind of fast, but who cares? I couldn't believe that I already had become friends with the hottest girl in school. This day was going to be so amazing.

Third period was the worst. Geometry. Like what exactly can I do with this in my life? Sitting in class for two hours learning why a triangle can be proved as a triangle. What does that even mean? The hour of math class went by so slow. At the end of class I walked up to the teacher and asked her for help on a homework problem. I know, homework on the first day, couldn't get any worse, can it? I headed for the door but a girl stopped me while I was trying to escape the classroom. She said her name was Maddie. We started talking and she was really funny so I knew her and I would be great friends. I was always the jock at my school so it's no surprise that all the girls were all over me on the first day. We went to lunch together and we sat down and talked the whole time. She was really cool and really talented. She showed me all the artwork she was working on. I knew she'd be an artist one day. She was so impressed by her own work and I thought it was great that she liked her work. Many artists don't find the talent in their own work and I respected her because I'm a sports guy and I don't have any artistic talent so it was cool to see such great artwork.

The bell rang because it was time for gym. I told Maddie I would walk her to class and while we were walking down the hallway together I looked behind me and all of the sudden she was gone. I turned back and she had stopped to get a drink so she was a few steps behind me now. Lauren, the hot girl from earlier was walking toward me. I got really happy as she looked at me, giving me a really flirty smile. She walked past me and looked at her friends and said "aw look at how ugly she is, why's she even here?". I turned around once again and saw Maddie's face turn to a complete state of depression. I waited for her to catch up and I asked her what was going on. She said that Lauren had been harassing her for months and wouldn't leave her alone and she went on talking about all the things she's said to her. I said I was sorry but I didn't want to get involved and screw up my chances of dating the hottest girl in school, lucky me right? I kept walking and eventually made it to gym. I had totally forgotten what happened.

Gym, sorry I mean P.E. (my teacher would get upset if we called it gym and not P.E.) was really fun. I was the football and soccer captain back at my old school so I fit right in with the popular, athletic guys. I made a lot of new friends and I even talked to the coach about soccer tryouts. I was so happy that my first day was going so smoothly. At school, ever see a kid become so popular, so quickly? That kid was me. Naturally I would be surprised if anyone didn't like me to be honest.

Maddie texted me to meet her at the front doors after school so I did. I walked up to her and I could tell she had been crying. I asked her what was wrong and she said she didn't want to talk about it. I understood. I hate talking about my feelings too. We walked outside to where our moms were waiting to pick us up. Lauren had followed us outside and came up to Maddie. She threw a package of makeup at her and said "use this, maybe you can fix your face with it". This abuse had been going on for a very long time but no one ever stopped it. My heart broke for Maddie but I didn't say anything. Now I realize how stupid I was. Lauren asked if I wanted to walk with her so I did. We walked to our cars and she gave me a goodbye hug. I felt so excited and happy that this girl was actually giving me attention. I was used to it but it was still all I could think about.

Maddie called me later that night and asked if we could talk. I said sure. We talked for an hour and all of the sudden she went silent. She then started crying. Apparently Lauren was harassing Maddie online as well. She would call her a slut and a whore and at one point told her to just kill herself. It seems like something out of the "Mean Girls" movie, but nope. This was Maddie's life. Maddie didn't know what to do so she just deleted her social media to avoid future harassment, but I could still tell that it was tearing her up inside.

Lauren called me so I hung up with Maddie and answered her call. Maddie got upset that I left, but I didn't really care. I know this sounds insensitive, but at the time it didn't matter to me. All my attention was on Lauren. I wanted to talk to her and see if I could ask her out on a date. We talked for six hours and I ended up nervously asking her out on a real date. She said yes. I was so happy but I wasn't very surprised. Who wouldn't want to date me? I went to bed with a huge smile on my face.

I woke up to police sirens and lights. They were at my house again, along with the EMTs. My sister had a pretty serious stomach and heart issue and had to be taken to the hospital quite often. It was stressful but she always turned out okay. I think that's why I got so attached to Lauren. My parents were always focusing on my little sister that they rarely had any time for me. My sister was taken by the ambulance to the hospital. I started getting ready for school and my aunt came over and picked me up because my dad and mom were going to the hospital to be with my sister.

Ahh, the second day of school. Always easier than the first. So much less stress. I went to first period. First period study hall with Mrs. Hendricks. She was cool but if you said hi, she'd start talking to you about all these things that had nothing to do with school. I said hi. That mistake was made only once. She started talking about her husband and how grumpy he gets and why her sister won't talk to her and just all this family drama. After talking to her for five minutes, I walked over to where Maddie was sitting. When I got there I saw Lauren's table and she had motioned for me to go sit with her. We had decided that we'd go on a date that night, out to dinner. She said she was excited for our date that night. I was too, believe me.

We dumped our lunch and waited for the bell. It finally rang so we got up and left. Maddie was walking in front of us and Lauren, out of nowhere, kicked her book bag which caused Maddie to trip. I couldn't help but laugh. I knew I shouldn't of but I couldn't help it. She had fallen right on the floor in the lobby. Over 100 people saw it and everyone started laughing at her. Lauren looked over at her and said "that's what you get for sending him those nudes you slut". I didn't know what she was talking about so I asked Lauren what was going on. She told me that Maddie sent her ex boyfriend a couple of nude pictures of herself while Lauren and this guy were still dating. I was surprised that Maddie would do something like that, I expected that behavior more from Lauren to be completely honest. I eventually made it to my next class, science. I hugged Lauren and said goodbye.

Maddie was in this class with me. When she entered the room, she knew that everyone was talking about her. Lauren had told all her friends about the nude pictures that were sent and now everyone in school knew about them. She quietly walked to her desk. She didn't really talk a lot as she was very shy in front of other teens. Ugh, the dreadful class. It was a lab day and we had to partner up for our first project. I hate partnering up on projects. One person always ends up doing most of the work and I knew I'd be that person. I partnered up with Maddie because she was the only person I knew in the class and Lauren went to the office so I couldn't choose her. We actually worked pretty well together. We finished it before anyone else in the class did.

We had finally sat down to relax and out of the blue she asked me why everyone was judging her so bad for the pictures. I told her that she really shouldn't have done it even though he asked for it and I told her to just ignore it. She told me she was really upset and didn't want to continue dealing with this. She said "everyone thinks I'm this awful person now and I only made one mistake and I can't get past it when everyone keeps talking about me. I just wanted that guy to like me, I didn't think he'd show all his friends my pictures". I said to her "well what do you want to do about it?". She didn't respond back. I could see the pain in her eyes. She stated she'd rather be dead than have to deal with it anymore. I didn't think she was serious so I just started talking about something different. I get very uncomfortable talking about feelings and death and stuff like that. I'm so scared of dying so I try to avoid that conversation at all costs.

My phone started ringing so I answered it. It was my dad calling me to say that I'm getting out early from school today to see my sister in the hospital. I wanted to see her so I packed up my stuff and told my teacher I was leaving early. I said bye to Maddie and told her that if she needed me tonight to call me. I walked to the office to sign out and my dad came in and got me. We went to the hospital and went in and saw my sister. She was doing very well and she was being so brave. I was so proud of her. She's only twelve.

It got closer to the time of my date with Lauren so I told my dad I had to go home to shower and stuff. We went home and I took a shower and changed into some date appropriate clothes. I bought a new cologne, the one Lauren said she liked. It was a good smell though. I took one last look in the mirror and I thought I looked good so I left. We met Lauren at an Italian restaurant. We were going to have a nice dinner so we could talk and get to know each other more. I walked into the restaurant and she was already there. The waitress took me to my table and then it hit me. The most beautiful girl in the world was right in front of me. I was so lucky to be on a date with this girl that my head couldn't even wrap itself around it. I told her how gorgeous she looked and she told me how handsome I looked.
We ordered dinner and started talking about life. I told her how I was really excited for the new Transformers movie to come out and she told me about new hairstyles she wanted to try and it was just a good night. We connected well.

But then I was interrupted by a phone call. Actually 19 phone calls, all from Maddie. I texted her back and said "I'm on a date with Lauren, I'll talk to you later." She replied "you said you'd be there for me tonight, I have no one else, please…". I answered back "I'm sorry, I'll talk to you later." I then turned my phone off. We ate our dinner and I paid the bill being the gentleman that I am. We left and when I was just about to hug her bye, she kissed me and said goodnight. She then walked to her car. I just stood there in shock. I couldn't believe that just happened. I got in my car and my sister was there, she had just gotten out of the hospital. I gave her a hug and told my family about the amazing night I had.

I finally got home and I was so tired that I just went to bed. I totally forgot to message Maddie. I had a good night sleep and I woke up for my third day of school at my new school which I was really starting to love. I got up and realized I totally forgot to do my homework. I quickly showered and changed my clothes and I wrote down random answers just so I could say I did it. I left for school, but I was really tired today which wasn't normal for me. My dad pulled into the parking lot and multiple police cars and fire trucks flew past us going at least 70 miles per hour. They were all heading past the school. Maddie lived near the school and for some reason I got a really weird feeling but didn't think anything of it. When I got to first period I had realized Maddie wasn't there. Then I remembered I forgot to text her. I texted her asking where she was and got no response. A kid in my class asked me if I knew what happened. I said no and he stated "Lauren got a couple of her friends to beat on that girl and that's why the police were here at school." I couldn't believe it. I wouldn't believe it. I knew Lauren wouldn't have done that to Maddie. I figured her friends just didn't like her or something. I texted Maddie again and told her that I hoped she was okay, again no response. The day went by pretty slow. I didn't feel so well because I think I caught a cold from someone.

Later that day I saw Lauren and I asked her what the hell was going on with her and Maddie and she just looked at me with a blank face. I asked her again and she said she didn't know. She said she had no part in what happened. I said okay and I believed her. That night, Maddie finally called me. I answered her immediately and asked if she was okay. She said Lauren and her friends messaged her some pretty hateful, mean things and told her to just kill herself and do the world and school a huge favor. I didn't believe that she would say that so I called Maddie a liar and I hung up the phone. I called Lauren and told her what happened. She said she'd never say mean things like that to someone and I knew she was telling the truth.

The next day, Maddie wasn't in school. I was still very mad at her so I didn't really care. All of the sudden the principal came on the speaker and said the school was going to have an assembly next period. I was excited because I would be able to miss math which is always a great thing. It finally came time for the assembly. I walked to the auditorium and sat next to Lauren. People were crying and hugging and I was really confused as to what was going on. The principal walked to the front of the room and said "guys I'm sorry to have to inform you this, but one of your classmates is no longer with us and her parents asked us to tell you that she took her own life last night." I immediately got a sharp pain in my chest and I knew it was Maddie. Tears started rushing down my face. I looked at Lauren and she just had a blank stare. I couldn't stop crying along with the rest of my classmates. I kept asking myself questions like "Why did this happen?" and "Why didn't you stop her?".

The principal kept talking about what happened and I didn't know what to do so I called my dad and he picked me up. My family knew what had happened.

Apparently someone told them. I got home and my mom was trying to hug me and comfort me, but I just ran up to my bed and cried hysterically. I fell asleep on my bed and woke up several hours later. Lauren had called me and left a message. In it she explained how she didn't want to be with me anymore and that she found someone else she has feelings for. I couldn't believe it.

It was the day of Maddie's funeral. I got no sleep so I was as tired as could be. My family came along with me and we sat in the back of the church during the ceremony. At the end while everyone was leaving some woman came up to me and asked "are you Paul?". I replied "yes I am". It was Maddie's mom. She had given me a letter. I ran to my car quickly and opened it. It read:

Dear Paul,

I don't know what I'm going to say in this letter but I'm going to try my very best. I didn't mean for this to happen. He was a football player and he was really popular and he gave me attention that no one else gave me and I liked it. He asked for some pictures so I just sent them to make him happy. I really didn't think he'd show all of his friends and that the whole school would see them. When I met you I thought I finally met someone who cared about me. We had so much in common and I thought you really cared about me. You said you'd be there for me, but you weren't and that's okay. I understand. I've never really been anything worth fighting for. I just couldn't deal with all of this anymore. Lauren and her friends wouldn't leave me alone and I can't go to school everyday wondering what people are saying about me. I'm so sorry Paul. I really did like you. I hope your relationship with her goes well. Good luck in school. Bye Paul.

~Maddie

I realized now...this is all my fault. I could have prevented this but I didn't. I chose some stupid girl over my friend. I let her down. I told her I cared and I did nothing to show it to her. I'm so sorry Maddie... I can't believe I did this to you.

It was Monday which meant school again. I walked into school. But this time I wasn't excited, scared, anxious or anything. I had no feelings. I hadn't showered in days and my clothes were still on from a couple days ago and I didn't care. I had no energy to change my clothes or do anything. I missed her like crazy and there was nothing I could do about it. I walked into my study hall and everyone just looked at me like they were disappointed in me. One kid even looked at me with the dirtiest look I've ever seen. That night my sister came into my room and just looked at me. She stood there and whispered something to me. "You always told me to stand up to bullies and to defend your friends when they need help, but you didn't. Am I not supposed to either?"

Paul took his life later that night.

—End of Story—

I personally know how it feels to be bullied and I know the possible outcomes when someone is bullied. Many of you will probably think this is a made up, stupid story to teach kids a lesson on why not to bully. That is simply not true. This was based on a true story. Now, while I was not a part of this story, I do understand bullying and how it works. There is only one word to describe bullying. Disgusting. If you think it's cool to bully, pick on, abuse or make fun of other teens then you are sadly mistaken. I've witnessed so much bullying over the course of my life and everytime I see it it makes my blood boil. I understand that you may feel insecure and that's why you might bully, but instead of picking on others, worry about yourself.

The sad fact is that bullying especially in the 12-18 age range can lead to suicide. That has to stop. We all have to come together and be nice. What exactly is the reason to be mean to someone, especially over social media? I see so many people commenting on social media statuses and pictures of people they don't even know just to be rude and cruel. Why? Why would you do that? Leave them alone. They don't need to be bullied just because you're having a bad day. Everyday I see comments like 'you're ugly' or stuff similar to that. It's so cruel. Instead I challenge all of you to comment something nice on someone's picture or on someone's status. Be a good person.

You never know what someone is going through behind closed doors. The rude comment you just said to her might be the last straw she had left before she gives up. Bullying. Why do we do it? Are you comfortable being the reason someone is hurting, or are you comfortable being the reason someone tries to end their pain?

The following piece of writing was written by talented author Aimee Eddy who is also a director for the National Youth Internet Safety and Cyberbullying Task Force.

It's Up To You To Stand Up

I know you're under a lot of pressure in school. Everyone wants to be accepted. Some will do anything to get into the popular crowd, even if it means picking on the kid who is a bit awkward or different. You might say things that you feel bad about just so the rest of the kids will like you, but being popular isn't important. Don't judge or taunt others just to be a part of the "in" crowd. The popular crowd isn't worth hurting others for.

Follow your heart. If your heart says it's wrong, do not do it just because everyone else is. Be the first person to sit with the classmate whom no one will sit next to. Take the first steps to get to know the kid everyone taunts. Be the one to stand up to your friends and say, "enough is enough." Tell a teacher, your parent, or the principal about the bullying. Remember, words hurt. It's up to you to take a stand against bullying.

If you take the time to get to know the person being bullied, you might find out you have a lot in common. You might find he or she is not so different from you and you could make a new friend, a true friend. Many who are facing teasing just need someone to lean on, to talk to, and to show them they matter. You can be the one to do this.

If you talk to the one being put down, your friends may turn their backs on you. Those people were never your real friends in the first place. A true friend sticks beside you no matter what. He or she will support your choices; he or she will cherish your uniqueness, and allow you to be yourself. A true friend will never ask you to be something you're not in order to fit in, or to harm others to be part of the crowd. You might just find the person whom others turn their back on can be a real friend.

Be you. Don't fight to be in the popular crowd. Accept everyone despite his or her disabilities, weight, clothing style, hair style, and so on. If you see someone being bullied, be the first one to speak up or get the person help. Be a beautiful, wonderful individual who cares for others and stands up to bullies. #endbullying

Section 30
Loneliness

I have lived my entire life with no more than five true friends at a time. Right now I have one best friend and that's pretty much it, but I'm totally okay with that. I do have friends, but not many that I fully trust and can actually say that I truly love them. I've been blessed with an amazing best friend so I am extremely lucky, however I wasn't always that lucky. Before last year, I truly had no one. People will say they were there for me, but in reality when I needed them they were nowhere to be found. Many friends got sick of my depression so they left my life, but that's okay. It can be hard and confusing for others to understand and sometimes they just don't care so they end up leaving you, but again that's okay. I don't want anyone in my life who truly doesn't want to be there. Want to leave? Bye! I have grown to not really care if people want to leave. I'm doing amazing things with my life right now, so I don't need to deal with the immaturity that some people feel the need to give out.

Loneliness is a feeling we often try to get rid of, even if it means hanging out with people we probably shouldn't hang out with. Don't hang out with or become friends with people just because you're lonely. Often times by doing that, you'll meet fake friends or bad influences or people that will take advantage of you. Instead, wait. Make friends slowly. Talk to some classmates or some people that do sports with you or are in band or choir with you. Find people that share similar qualities and like the same things as you.

I was in your shoes, very lonely. I had no friends. I never hung out with anyone and I never went anywhere really. But that's okay. I turned out just fine. If you feel lonely and like you don't have friends, it's okay. I know it's a tough feeling to have but you will get through it! Get out there and make some friends, whether it be online (only if they live near you) or in school. There's always someone who will make a great friend to you, and I learned that, but it took a while. Remember, having one true, honest best friend is way better than three hundred "friends".

Section 31
Depression and Sadness

I'm sorry you are going through depression. I understand how awful it is. It's like going through a constant battle with yourself. It really can take a toll on you and it causes you to act like a totally different person sometimes. Here I'm going to give some tips and talk about how to work through depression based on what I've gone through and what I've learned.

First let's look at the symptoms of depression, if you think you might have it or if you are too scared to admit that you might have it. First things first. Don't be scared! You aren't crazy and depression is not something to be embarrassed about. It's not your fault that you feel this way, but make sure to reach out and get help. It will be much easier for you to get through, trust me! If you feel hopeless, worthless, and irritable, and if you find less interest in activities you used to love then you might be going through depression. Also, if you've had a change in your sleeping pattern then it might be possible that you are depressed.

Appetite issues, less energy, and aches and pains are also symptoms of depression.

When I first became depressed I had many symptoms. I started getting very sad over little things. I started sleeping way more than usual. I started to eat a lot less if anything at all and I started getting annoyed very easily at the smallest of things. I began to feel very worthless and I lost energy for everything. After a few weeks I began getting very tired all the time after doing almost no activities that would cause me to become tired. I could sleep for thirteen hours straight, miss school, and still be extremely tired. That's part of how my depression worked in high school. I also began getting extreme pain in my muscles and chest due to depression and from having anxiety attacks. The most important thing to remember is that not everyone has the same depression. We all have different stages of it and we all have different symptoms. Some of us have many while others have very few if any.

Don't get depression confused with sadness. If you failed a test and are sad because of it then that doesn't mean you have depression. It means you are just going through a stage of sadness. When the sadness doesn't go away, that's when you should talk to your doctor about depression. Depression is also common with teens that attempt suicide as well so it's very important that you get professional help before it leads to something worse. Remember this though, if you have depression, you're still you! You aren't crazy or stupid and you are not to blame at all for having depression. I used to think people would think I am crazy for being depressed. That's not true. People judge when they don't understand or are misinformed and that often happens with depression and mental illnesses.

School performance, family life and siblings, social status with peers, sexual orientation, sports, and college can each have a major effect on how a teen feels.

Teen Depression Symptoms

- Withdrawal from friends and/or family
- Headaches and/or stomachaches
- Fatigue and/or pain in muscles/joints
- Difficulty concentrating in school or at home
- Difficulty making decisions

- Excessive guilt over small issues/situations
- Irresponsible behavior (forgetting obligations, being late for classes, skipping school, missing sports practices)
- Appetite problems/Sleeping problems
- Memory loss
- Constant nervous feeling
- Constantly thinking about death or dying
- Rebellious behavior (drugs, drinking, smoking, vaping, and involving yourself in peer pressure)
- Feeling of hopelessness or worthlessness
- Staying awake at night and sleeping during the day or sleeping for long periods of time
- Sudden drop in grades at school or in college
- Getting involved in promiscuous sexual activity

The following piece of writing was written by talented author Aimee Eddy who is also a director for the National Youth Internet Safety and Cyberbullying Task Force.

How do you describe depression? Would you describe it as a dark cloud over your soul, an internal hell, or an endless road into darkness? Is depression to you the blues once in a while or something that just won't go away? There is a difference between having sad days and having a serious illness. The blues once in a while is not depression. To me, depression is a dark hole you can't get out of. It's an illness that you're stuck in and just can't shake. It's there night and day.

Depression followed me throughout my school years. I can't remember exactly when I started falling down the dark hole. Was it in first grade when my teacher called me a retard or the years that followed when I was told I'd never be anyone? Was it in seventh grade when my uncle was killed or the years after when I stopped talking? I think I started falling through all of those events. Slowly grade by grade I fell further and further down the hole.

It was my senior year of high school that I fell to the bottom of the hole. I fell all the way down when my cousin was killed in a car accident. I fell so far down I felt like there was no way out. I tried to climb the walls of my hole. I grasped at the roots of hope, but they withered away. I slipped back down to the bottom of my hole. The darkness surrounded me and crept into my soul. The walls of the hole seemed like they were closing in on me.

The things that once gave me joy no longer did, the nights seemed endless, I was lucky to keep food down, sadness smothered me, I couldn't concentrate, and my life started to seem hopeless. I started to injure myself and plan my death. I couldn't see beyond the dark hole. I was trapped. My only way out was to end it all. I thought my family would be happier if I was gone. I thought I'd finally be freed.

I was wrong.

In therapy I started learning ways to change my thinking such as changing my negative thought, "I am a hopeless loser," to "I am strong and I am a winner." Then I started seeing a psychiatrist and he put me on antidepressants. The roots of hope became stronger and I began to pull myself up. With one root and one lifeline at a time I edged my way up from the bottom of the hole. My lifelines were therapy, medication, and support from my family. I couldn't do it alone.

It wasn't easy.

I had to change my thinking, I had to dig up the past and patch up some deep wounds. I had to tell my therapist my deepest secrets. I had to dig my heels into the side of my hole and climb to the light above. I had to search deep within myself and find determination to find recovery. I had to want to reach the light and I had to want it so bad I could think of nothing else.

No matter how you describe your depression, there is a way out. You need to be willing to take the first step of accepting your illness. Then you have to be willing to fight and do what is necessary to reach recovery. You can't do it alone. Find help. Build a support system, go to therapy, get the right medication and find the determination to get better.

Suicide isn't the answer. It might seem like an easy way out, but it is actually giving up on yourself. You can get better. You can be happy again. You can reach recovery and learn to control your illness. The fight is in you. Look deep in your soul and find your hidden strength and fight. Fight for you, fight for happiness, fight for a better life, and fight with all that's in you.

You can do it.

I fought with all of my strength and now I am standing at the top of the hole. I have found happiness. I'm not cured, but I have a strong support system to get me through the rough times. I'm also too strong to allow myself to fall back down the hole of depression. Come on, you can do it. You can stand at the top with me.

~End of Story~

I used to feel so hopeless and like I would never get better. I felt the same things you are feeling now, so trust me when I say this. If you work for it, you can get better. I mean that. I worked toward getting better and over time it pays off with hard work and effort.

You won't get cured in three days or even three months. It's going to be a stressful uphill battle, but that's okay because you're really strong and you can set your mind to anything you want to accomplish.

Don't give up and take the easy way out. Get through it and prove everyone doubting you wrong. You can and will do this. I know it seems hopeless and like I'm wrong, but one day you will realize that I'm right when I say this. Get better and focus on yourself! You are much stronger than you think you are.

Section 32
Eating Disorders

I've gone through a few eating disorders throughout my life. They honestly are awful. It's a feeling of hating your body so much to the point where you eat too little or too much. It's extremely challenging to get through eating disorders. Many people feel that you have to be extremely skinny to have an eating disorder, but that's very far from the truth. I'm six feet tall and weigh about one hundred and seventy-five pounds which is not a lot for my height but I'm also nowhere near being underweight to the point of starvation so most people don't feel that I could possibly have an eating disorder.

Also, I'm a guy. Many people think men can't get eating disorders, but they can. I've lived with atypical anorexia nervosa (eating almost nothing, but there's no change in weight), night eating syndrome and binge eating disorder (eating nothing during the day and consuming it all at once, usually during the night). I still struggle with this a lot, but it doesn't really affect my life like it used to. Now it's kind of just normal for people in my life to see me not eat. It's not okay or healthy by any means, but it's just how I have always been. I don't hate my body anymore, but I had an eating disorder for so long that I just became used to not eating. I never eat breakfast. I never eat lunch. In fact I typically never eat before 5pm. I usually eat dinner, depending on if I'm hungry on that day.

When this all first started it was very hard to deal with. People seriously judged me. I'd be out with someone eating, and people wouldn't understand why I couldn't eat. And it's hard to explain so usually I'd try to eat a little just so I could say I ate something. That wouldn't work though because then I'd get judged for eating a small amount so it was just a lose-lose situation. People would laugh at me sometimes, which I never understood. You laugh at someone for not eating because it makes them physically sick?

Eating disorders do not define who you are. It's just a roadblock that you will overcome. It all takes time. You won't get better in five days, it'll take a while. We all have our own battles that we deal with everyday and eating disorders are just battles that we need to work through. And when we do we will start to see the light at the end of the tunnel. The light is always there, even in our darkest days. My eating disorder was one of the hardest things I've ever gone through, but it helped form the person I am today. It showed me who I really was and more importantly it showed me that I am worth it. I am loved and I deserve to love myself. You all deserve to love yourself, because you are all perfect in your own ways. We all have flaws, but that's what makes us who we are and that can't be changed. If you're battling through an eating disorder, then take baby steps. You will get through it, even if you believe you can't. I never thought I'd get over it so I understand how you are feeling. But I am here telling you that you can and will get through your eating disorder if you fight hard enough.

Because of my eating disorders, I used to become so depressed that I would find myself self loathing on every little thing that I didn't like about myself and my body. I'd spend hours and hours daily making lists of the things I needed to work on and the things that just weren't right about my body. This constant battle in my head left me with the feeling of never feeling good enough. I'd toss and turn in bed some nights wondering what I could do to just see myself as perfect.

That was my biggest mistake. There really is no definition or idea of perfection. No one is by definition perfect, because we all have flaws. Our flaws are what make us who we are meant to be. As a society, we constantly think about what's wrong with us and if people will see our flaws and weaknesses. We don't take time to look at how strong we are, how talented we are, and how intelligent we are. Those are the true important qualities of being human.

I used to become so depressed from my low self esteem that I would constantly self harm and I'd constantly hurt myself just so I could take a break from all the thoughts I had about myself. It became so serious that I eventually found a dislike in food. Weeks later, I found myself eating very little amounts of food just in hopes of possibly liking myself once again. This went on for several months and during those months I felt very empty, and broken, and like nothing else mattered, but what I looked like. Self harm has a strong connection to eating disorders because they both are usually results of someone finding flaws in themselves and not knowing how to handle it. Also from going through stress or a traumatic event and not knowing how to handle that as well. So many people are judged daily for who they are, what their body looks like, and what they eat. I will never understand why some people feel the need to send shame and hate to people living with eating disorders. As someone who has been through it, I know how hard it is and how much of a challenge it is to get through.

The truth is that your looks are simply that, your looks. What you look like does not define you. It doesn't define your character, your personality, or why you're likable. Having an eating disorder was one of the hardest things I eventually realized that my eating disorder does not define me. I can get better. I can feel better about myself. And most importantly, I can be me.

I thought that I could just eat again and be better in a week. It actually took me two years to work through my eating disorder and that's okay. The problem of today is that some people feel that they will get better so quickly and when they don't, they stop trying. Whether it's an eating disorder or whether it's self harm, it still is a difficult roadblock that will need time to heal. Getting past a difficult life roadblock takes time. It may take three months or it might take five years, but either one of those are perfectly okay. We all work through things at a different pace and that's what makes us, us. Always remember that your eating disorder does not and will never define who you are as a person. Having an eating disorder means that you're a very strong person who just hit a roadblock and needs a little push to get back on track. You are never alone. Nearly eight million people are currently living with an eating disorder. We, as a country have to come together to realize, to understand, and to educate ourselves about eating disorders. Nearly four percent of college aged females live with bulimia right now. That's a large number that needs to raise attention so we can become more educated on eating disorders.

If you're working through an eating disorder, then I am so incredibly proud of you. It takes hard work and lots of effort to work through it.

Don't be embarrassed. Tell someone whether it be a friend or family member. Seek out help or treatment. The first step to getting better is realizing you want to get better! Try eating breakfast daily as this can help you be more prepared for the day. Try eating small amounts of food to start. Eat a small breakfast and lunch to start off. Don't just stop eating and don't start eating too much either. And remember, you're beautiful in your own body and you are the only one who has to realize it. You will get through your eating disorders as it's a working process. I'm still not totally through it yet either. You may relapse and binge eat, or try throwing up your food, but don't take it out on yourself. Get back on your feet and back into that pattern. Realize you made a mistake and don't it let happen again. We all have breaking points, but what's important is moving on from relapse and getting better. You're perfect just as you are.

For Parents

It is very common for teenagers with eating disorders to not even be aware that they have a problem. If you suspect that your child has an eating disorder, they may not even realize it themselves. They may not see that they're eating less or more and they may not understand that they're doing it.

If you find that your child has abnormal weight changes, if you find that food is always missing in your house, if your teen avoids family meals such as dinner, or if you see them have an extreme focus on their appearance then it may be possible that your child is suffering from an eating disorder. I'd suggest contacting their doctor, therapist, or school counselor so you have the correct tools to aid your child so they don't feel judged.

Section 33
Self Harm and Cutting

About a year and a half ago I started cutting. I didn't do it for attention. In fact I tried covering my arms and wrists just so people wouldn't see it. I cut because I felt there was too much emotional stress and abuse going on in my life that I could no longer handle it. I began taking it out on myself by cutting. Every time I cut it generally got worse. Most times scars were left behind, but remember your scars only show how strong you are for being here. Don't feel embarrassed as it's nothing to be embarrassed over. I did get bullied a lot if people saw my cuts or my scars healing. The main reason for the bullying is because other teens didn't understand why I would do that and they thought it was very stupid. Almost everyone thought I only did it for attention. But in the end, who really cares what those people think?

I cut for over a year until I realized my self worth and I slowly stopped doing it. I have had a couple relapses where I'd feel depressed and would get a razor and cut my skin again. Relapses are nothing to be ashamed of. You aren't perfect. You are human. It happens to us all. Just remember that it isn't good and that you are stopping the cutting to feel better in the future. It becomes very addicting, trust me I know. Cutting isn't the only way to harm yourself. Some people take drugs, or get high, or try to get drunk, but I've never done that. I've been peer pressured a lot but I still never did it. I've never taken drugs, or smoked and I've actually never drank alcohol so I can't relate to that at all. I just feel that getting high or drunk may make you feel better in the moment but it won't ever help in the long run. If you're trying to get clean from drugs, good for you! I'm really proud of you because it's a very hard thing to do and I'm proud you took the path to get better and that's something to be seriously proud of!

One common misconception about self harm is that people only self harm to commit suicide. This is very false. The majority of people who self harm don't actually want to kill themselves. They are just tired of the pain and are tired of being alone. Sometimes self harm can be a sign of a suicide attempt though so self harm should be taken seriously either way.

Self harm is never something to joke about. It isn't a joke. It's someone who is need of dire help and doesn't know who or what to turn to. When I began self harming, one of my parents actually wanted to ground me when they found out about it. This is truly disgusting to me. If your kid is hurting themselves then it's a cry for a help. If you ground them or blow it off then what kind of person are you? Talk to them and see what you can do to help. Support them and let them know you aren't mad at them, because why would you be? It isn't their fault and they just feel lost and aren't sure what to do. I know it has to be stressful for parents dealing with this. But always remember, do not blame your kid. Give them support because that's what they need the most. I get that it's tough to watch your child harm themselves. It's got to be hard for people to witness someone close to them purposely damaging their skin.

For Parents

Don't ask your teen lots of questions. Most times, teens self harm because they're struggling with how to reach out for help so they harm themselves because they aren't sure how to deal with their emotions. Asking why will not give you the answers you're looking for. Plus if your child isn't sure why they're cutting, you'll push them away and that will only make them feel uncomfortable and ashamed of themselves.

Do not ignore it. Like I said earlier, self injury usually isn't a sign of suicide, but oftentimes teens self harming may be thinking about suicide, so it's extremely important to take it very seriously and offer help so they know you're there for them. It may be extremely beneficial if you reach out to local therapists and ask them how you should talk to your child. It may be best if your child visits a therapist or counselor so that they can get professional help.

Parents are encouraged to reach out to the National Youth Internet Safety and Cyberbullying Task Force or the Crisis Text Line where you'll be assisted on how to help your child through self injury. If your teen or child is actively attempting suicide, dial 911 immediately. Do not wait or assume it's nothing.

Section 34
Relapsing

The number one thing to remember is to not blame yourself. That will only lead to more relapses which won't be good. Whether it's because of an eating disorder, or depression, or self harm; when you have been doing much better then it suddenly gets worse and your mental state gets worse, that is a relapse. For example, when I stopped cutting I was clean from it for a few months. Then one day I had a very bad, emotional day so I had a relapse and I cut again. I had to think about what I had done and while I was very disappointed in myself I knew it was okay and that I could do better the next time. I was right. Many people relapse and it's okay to relapse and make a mistake. We all make mistakes. Just make sure to seek help during a relapse because sometimes relapsing can be very serious and even more more dangerous than before.

Do not feel like you failed yourself. Be happy that you lasted so long without a relapse because that's a true accomplishment. That's also something to be very proud of. Now take your relapse and learn from it. Work harder this time and when the urges come back fight against them harder this time. Reach out for support and lean on your love ones. If you end up relapsing again, it's okay. You can't just get rid of it, never relapse, and just move on. I wish that were how it works but unfortunately, it isn't. Don't beat yourself up, because you're better than that.

One of the main things you have to learn to prevent relapse is being powerful. Whether you have had a cutting problem, or a drug addiction, or were an alcoholic, you have to learn how to be powerful and assertive towards yourself. I know it's hard to learn, but it has to be done. The more assertive and powerful you become, the more you'll be prone to saying no and stopping a possible relapse. After a relapse, create a new goal and a new relapse plan. If you relapsed after being clean for four months then make a plan saying you'll try to stay clean for eight months now and see how it goes. It is an uphill, bumpy road but you can do it but only if you truly believe it. Get back into your road to recovery and do not dwell on the past. You got this!

Section 35
Anxiety And Panic Attacks

Anxiety is something a lot of teens and college kids deal with. Between school, employment, dating, friends, family, and a social life, anxiety can definitely be part of a young adults everyday life. Anxiety typically causes someone to worry about different things, sometimes even things that seem so small and irrelevant. Sometimes, a person diagnosed with an anxiety disorder may worry about many different things, like me.

I have pretty bad anxiety. Growing up I'd worry about everything, legit everything. Everytime I heard about a disease, sickness, or cancer I would think that I had it. It would consume my thoughts and I'd worry for weeks until my brain decided that I didn't have whatever it was that I was all worked up about.

I was very young when I started recognizing the signs of an anxiety disorder. I always felt like something was off. I started feeling very restless, and I was constantly moving around while my thoughts would race very fast throughout my head.

I found myself constantly worrying about things that seemed so stupid to me, things that other people would laugh at. I'd find my mind racing while watching tv shows, reading books, or watching the news. If I watch a tv show where something happens like a boat crash, I'd then be completely terrified of going on a boat and I wouldn't. In twenty years, I have never flown on a plane, I've only been on a train and boat once, and I didn't do a lot of things that most teenagers would do. I was always worried about what could go wrong, even if the chances of it going wrong were almost nonexistent.

Anxiety attacks or panic attacks are often characterized as experiencing:
- A feeling of overwhelming fear
- Hot and cold flashes
- A feeling of going crazy or losing control
- Dizziness
- Heart palpitations
- A feeling that you're choking
- Trembling/Shaking
- Sweating

- Tingling feeling in hands and feet
- Shortness of breath
- Chest pressure or pain
- Feeling of extreme panic
- Weak in the joints
- Skin discoloration
- Numbness
- Dizziness/trouble staying still or standing up
- Emotional distress/crying
- Inability to calm yourself down
- Nausea
- Racing heart
- Butterflies in the stomach
- Vomiting

I became very fatigued all the time and I had a lot of trouble concentrating on things especially in school. The biggest struggle of anxiety is the difficulty in controlling your worrying behaviors. I started worrying about everything. From school, to being in public, to getting shot, to getting hurt, to airplanes, and even small things like the teacher calling out my name in class. I do have general anxiety which means I worry about almost anything, but I also have social anxiety which can be a lot tougher to live with, at least for me it was.

Social anxiety is intense anxiety or fear of being judged, negatively evaluated, or rejected in a social or performance situation. This means it can be hard for you to make friends, or speak in public, or even just walking into a crowded store. I became very worried that I was constantly being judged and that I would be embarrassed. I began worrying immensely about what others thought of me and if I'd say something that might offend them. I also started to avoid a lot of social situations like school activities, the lunch room, and even going to the mall. This caused me to struggle with making friends, doing sports, dating, and going out with any of the friends I did make. I didn't go out much with my friends because I was always worried, especially if new people I didn't know were going to be there too.

I think anxiety is something that a lot of people simply don't understand. My parents used to yell at me for not wanting to call people on the phone. I used to be very scared with calling people on the phone. I'd have an anxiety attack if I was forced to put in a pizza delivery order, but my parents didn't understand that. They just thought that I was being lazy. It really was that difficult for me to pick up the phone and call. You shouldn't judge people with an anxiety disorder. It may seem stupid to you, but to them it's very serious.

Don't let anxiety control your life, because in reality almost everything I've worried about happening never did. I have worried about having hundreds of life threatening illnesses and never had any of them. Bad things may happen to you. It happens to all of us, but you can't worry about the unknown. You may spend your entire life worried about something that will never even happen to you. I get that it isn't easy. Me saying 'don't worry' about something won't make the worries go away, but you have to reach out for help so you don't have to suffer through it alone.

Sometimes when you have anxiety you may experience panic or anxiety attacks. I've experienced some pretty scary panic attacks so it's understandable if you aren't sure on how to deal with them. My panic attacks usually consist of my heart racing, feeling weak and dizzy, extreme chest pain, trouble breathing, feeling a sense of being scared, and I also sweat a lot or have multiple cold chills at once. I also shake a lot. It's very scary because it truly feels like you are dying, especially when they are very severe panic attacks.

If you are having one, stay calm. It's harder said than done, I know. But make sure to breathe normally. Don't try to breathe differently to attempt to feel better. Take slow deep breaths. It's extremely important to keep your airways open and unblocked during an anxiety attack. If you start shaking, sit down and try to think about something that calms you down or put some music on. Music was a huge lifesaver for me. It would help me feel relaxed and I'd focus on the lyrics of the songs, rather than whatever I was worried about.

The most important thing is if you are in public, take a break. If you are in class then tell your teacher you need to go to the bathroom or that you need to go to the nurse. There's no reason to feel embarrassed about a panic attack, but it would be safer for you to leave the crowded space because that might be a cause for your panicking in the first place. If you have been having a lot of panic attacks lately, maybe it's time for a quick one day vacation or a quick break from life to relax for a day. If your anxiety is serious, I'd highly recommend visiting a school counselor or an adult you trust. It's not safe to keep it to yourself and pretend like it doesn't exist.

Section 36
Suicide And Suicide Attempts

Suicide is the one word that no one really likes talking about, but it is something that needs to be talked about because it's very serious and tragic. Teen suicide is one of the leading causes of death and it's something that I tirelessly try to help teenagers with. Suicide is something that really hits home with me. I had a couple suicide attempts and I lost my best friend to suicide as well as three other friends. It's a tough subject but I really want to discuss it to possibly help others in the future. The following section does talk about suicide in detail so if this triggers you, skip to the next section.

Sadly, suicide is the answer to many teenage issues and it's a very unfortunate event to occur. It can destroy the lives of family members, teachers, friends, and so on. Teenagers attempt suicide for many reasons. Maybe because they dislike themselves, or because they were raped or abused, and maybe even because they feel lonely and don't feel like they have another option besides ending their life.

Obviously as you heard from many people, suicide is never the answer. Hearing that from peers, teachers, and even family really doesn't make an impact on a teens life. But maybe I can make an impact on your life because I've been in your shoes and I know almost exactly what you're feeling right now. Before my hospital visit I thought that suicide was the only way to escape my pain. That it would make everyone happy if I were just gone. I was sadly mistaken. Luckily I wasn't successful and I'm still here. If I had died I would not have been here to help all the teenagers I have helped so far. I would have made so many people feel awful about themselves for not being able to stop me. Even if you have no friends it still will affect classmates very drastically.

You may think no one cares about you, but you are wrong. There are people out there that would question their own life if you decided to take yours. Don't do that to them. Most importantly don't do that to yourself. A large portion of suicide attempts are failures, meaning that you do not die. You may however, be paralyzed or injured for the rest of your life now because of your attempt at suicide. Don't do that to yourself and your future. I felt like the most worthless person alive. I had no idea why I was alive and I felt I was doing the world a favor by leaving. In reality I am here for a reason. If you're suicidal, chances are you don't feel it will get better and you don't think life will ever get any better. This is understandable. I used to feel the same way and I still do once and awhile. But, life truly does get better. I promise. I know it doesn't seem like it will, but it does. I went through a ton and I thought it would never get better, but it did. It takes time! I had to go through months more of awful things, but it did finally improve. I started helping others and I started talking to teens across the world about depression, bullying, and suicide. And I started writing which has been going very well for me. I never thought I'd improve and I never thought my life would actually really go anywhere, but boy was I wrong. I know it's hard to believe, that life will get better, just hang on! You'll eventually see what I mean and you'll understand what I'm talking about right now.

If you feel suicidal then think about this. If you have a sibling then I bet you guys fight a ton. That's totally normal. But deep down, you probably do really love them and care about them. And as much as they pick on you and fight with you, they do love you. They would be totally lost if you committed suicide. So would your parents. Even if you have the most unsupportive parents in the world, it would still crush them. You may feel that no one cares about you, but I guarantee that you are wrong. There is someone who would be affected severely if you took your own life. I've felt what you are feeling so you can't say "well you just don't understand" because I really do understand. I didn't think anyone would care about me, but months later I now realize how many lives I would have destroyed if I actually was not here anymore.

Do not ever joke about suicide. Jokes about suicide are simply disgusting, mean, and disrespectful. Grow up and realize that your words hurt. Don't tell someone to kill themselves. This is the worst thing you could say to someone in my opinion. It's not a joke. What if you said something like that and they actually did kill themselves? How would you feel?

Suicide is not the answer. If you ever need help, reach out for it. There's so much love and support for you out there, trust me.

"I Killed Myself Yesterday"

My mom woke up really early this morning. For some reason, I think she could sense that something was wrong. I guess that's just a mom thing. She came out of her room and walked over to my door and banged on it trying to get me to wake up for school. She then walked over to my sister's door and banged on her door as well. Normally this is when I would wake up, but not today.

My mom walked downstairs to make breakfast for my sister and I. My dad usually made us breakfast, but he had to go into work really early because he had a busy day today. My sister ran down the stairs as fast as she could. She was only fourteen so she still got excited going to school every morning to see her friends and her favorite teachers. I wasn't so much of a school person. I didn't like sitting in classes all day waiting for the last bell to ring so I could leave.

My mom began wondering why I wasn't coming downstairs. I always came down before my sister so I think my mom thought that I was sick or something. She gave my sister her breakfast and then she walked upstairs into my room. She walked over and tried to wake me up, but there wasn't anything she could do. It was too late. She started getting really scared and I think it finally hit her. My mom fell to the floor hysterically screaming and crying. She was trying to wake me up. She kept screaming and asking how this could be happening. My sister ran up the stairs and into my room. She saw my mom hugging my body and she didn't understand what was going on. She started getting scared so she backed away a little bit. When she backed up, she stepped on something. She looked down to see what it was, only to find an empty pill bottle.

When I went to bed last night, I really thought that I could no longer handle living the life that I was given. I thought my only option was to kill myself, so that is exactly what I did.

My mom called my dad and my dad had no clue what she was saying because all she could do was cry. He raced home as fast as he could to find me laying there. He called 911, but there wasn't anything that the fire department could do. My mom kept screaming at them, trying to get them to save her baby, but it was too late. Every EMT, firefighter, and police officer rushed to my house to try to find a heartbeat or a pulse just somewhere. Unfortunately, they didn't find one.

Everyone started finding out at my high school. My first period teacher couldn't teach her class anymore. She kept blaming herself for yelling at me the day before. She thought that she had something to do with why I no longer was there in class. All my teachers felt this way. They all asked themselves what they could have done different. They thought they missed a sign that I needed help. I wish they knew that it wasn't their fault. I wish I could just tell them. My English teacher and I were very close. That night, she had gone to the bar to relieve the stress that my passing had caused her. She had been clean from drinking for over three years.

I think it hit my best friend harder than anyone else. She stared at the wall all day. She just wanted her best friend back. She kept blaming herself for not stopping me. She kept wondering why I wouldn't have told her what was going on in my head. She kept blaming herself for the fight we had last week. We had argued a lot the week prior and we had talked about going our own ways in the friendship even though we didn't mean it. She blamed herself for my choices. I wish I could tell you how much I love you. I wish I could tell you that you were the best person in my life. You were truly the only person that I could totally be myself around. I wish I could tell you that this wasn't your fault. I wish I could just talk to you one last time.

My sister didn't know what to do with herself. She looked up to me. She saw me as a role model. We had our fights and differences, but we really were inseparable. She didn't want to continue her life because I wasn't there anymore. She began self harming to deal with all of the stress that she had to go through at such a young age. She stopped eating and she stopped going to school. She had trouble getting out of bed and going outside. She eventually was diagnosed with two eating disorders and depression. She struggles everyday and she continues to struggle going forward. I wish I didn't do this. I need to be there for her. I need to be there to see her graduate. To see her get married. To meet her children. I just need to be there for her. She needs me, but I can't be there for her anymore.

My mom can't get the images out of her head. She can't get out of her bed because she fears that she will have to relive the trauma of losing her first child. My dad started drinking and he began going out late to deal with the stress. One night he was pulled over by the state police for drinking while intoxicated. Their marriage quickly broke and they both couldn't deal with living life without me. They both blamed themselves and each other for what happened. They had thought that they were the reason behind me taking my life. I didn't think they cared about me this much. I never really looked at all the people who cared about me. I constantly said that no one cared, but now I truly see that so many people cared about me. They just didn't know how to show it that well I guess. Now that I'm gone, I see all of these people that loved me so much. I wish I was still here to hug them all...

My soccer teammates struggled to continue their season without seeing me on the field. I had the solo in the fall choir concert, but my teacher couldn't give the solo to someone else. She kept thinking that I'd still be there to perform at the concert. I don't think that it hit her yet. People that I don't even know walk the hallways full of sadness because I'm no longer there. The school principal blamed himself for not stopping me, my ex girlfriend blamed herself for cheating on me, and my friends still cry everyday in class looking at the empty seat in the room.

I did matter. I was cared about. People did love me, but I just couldn't see it. I let my depression take over and I didn't think that I could fight through all the sadness and pain. I never wanted to cause all of these people pain. I never thought anyone would miss me. I wish that I just reached out for help. I wish I could have worked through this. I know I could have gotten better, but at the time I just couldn't deal with it all.

I never lived to see how successful I'd become in college. I never got to see the amazing job that I was offered four years later. I never knew that I'd meet an amazing girl who I'd soon marry and have kids with. I never knew that I'd become a New York Times best selling author. That was always my dream. I never thought that I was good enough, but I guess that I really was. I'd eventually start my own charity to help teens who have runaway from home. I am not sure why I decided to do this, but I won't ever find out. I also saved a child from an abusive home, whom I adopted shortly after, but I won't get to ever meet her. I wish I had known how successful I'd be. If only I had known. I never thought that someone like me could work through the depressing feelings that I faced everyday, but I guess I did. Unfortunately, I'll never be here to see any of it. I made a life ending decision just to stop temporary problems and feelings that I thought I couldn't control. I changed so many lives. I destroyed my friends and family, but I really didn't mean to do that. I thought that this would be the better decision for both me and everyone in my life. I really regret it. I wish I could do it all over again. But I can't because...

I killed myself yesterday.

~End of Story~

Teen Suicide Warning Signs
- Increased use of alcohol/drugs
- Telling loved ones goodbye
- Talking about feelings of hopelessness
- Isolating and withdrawing themselves
- Extreme changes in their appearance
- Talking about being a burden to others
- Acting highly anxious or agitated
- Acting reckless and taking risks
- Signs of severe depression

- Rage or uncontrolled anger
- Losing interest in things
- Trapped or desperate to escape an intolerable situation
- Suffers from low self-esteem
- Self harming behaviors
- Changes in sleeping and/or eating

For Parents

Offer help and listen to your child if you suspect that something is off with them. Don't ever ignore the problem. What you've noticed may be the teen's way of crying out for help. If you ignore the problem, the teen may make dangerous choices to get your attention. It's better to sit down and ask your child how they're doing then to ignore a serious problem.

Offer support, understanding, and compassion. Always remember, you don't need to solve the problem or give advice. Sometimes just caring and listening, and being nonjudgmental will help your teen reach out for help.

- Don't be scared to talk about suicide with your teen. Talking about suicide doesn't cause suicide, but avoiding the conversation may make it so you can't recognize how your child is feeling.
- Ask if your child has a plan for suicide and what the plan is. If he or she does, then seek professional help immediately or dial 911.
- If you suspect that your teen may be seriously struggling, remove lethal weapons from your home, such as guns and knives. Lock up pills, and be aware of the location of kitchen utensils, as well as ropes and belts, which can be used as means to commit suicide.
- A teen at risk of suicide needs immediate professional help. Do not ignore the problem or make excuses for your child. If your teenager is suicidal, reach out for help immediately such as by taking your child straight to the emergency room or by dialing 911 or your local police department.

I know that it seems difficult to reach out for help, but it might just change your life. I know that it seems easier to just give up, but you can't. You really have no idea where your life will go. In fact, most teens who attempt suicide and survive immediately regret doing it. I know that you feel it won't ever change. That it's easier to just give up. You may be giving up an amazing future that you can't even imagine. Pain is only temporary. Please keep fighting through your depression and mental illnesses. You're perfect just the way you are and don't let anyone tell you differently. I believe in you and I know that you can do this. Keep fighting. I know it may seem like you disappearing won't affect anyone in your life, but I can promise you that it will.

44,193 Americans die by suicide each year.

For every one suicide, twenty-five attempt suicide.

Pain doesn't last forever.

From one survivor to the next, it does get better.

You belong here. Keep fighting through the pain and sadness. Don't give up. You can do this. Stay strong.

Section 37
Things Not To Say To Someone Struggling

I get it. Hearing the same things over and over again really doesn't help anyone feel better. Most people are just trying to help and aren't too sure on what to say. Some things however, can be very rude and insensitive. Here's a list of things you shouldn't say to someone going through mental illnesses or a tough life situation.

You're just sad, it'll get better.
Get over it already, you'll be fine.
Grow up and act like an adult.
Depression isn't that bad.
Just snap out of it.
You have nothing to be depressed about.
You don't have it that bad.
Other people have it worse than you.
Depression isn't real. It's all in your head.
Depression is not a real illness.
Depression just means you're sad.
You're just being lazy.
You sleep too much. What's wrong with you?

You wouldn't be depressed if you just tried hard enough.
Depression isn't that bad.

No one chooses to have depression so it's not something that can just be changed. A depressed person can't just be happy if you they try hard enough. It takes a lot of work and effort to work through depression. Don't tear them down by saying those things to them. Sometimes it's hard to understand and it's hard to know what to say, but be supportive and make sure they know that you are there for them.

Don't say these things to someone with anxiety:

It's all in your head.
Just stop worrying.
Just man up and go do what you need to do.
You're just being a drama queen.
Grow up, it's not that hard to do.
What are you getting so upset about? It's not that big of a deal.
What's wrong with you? Just calm down already.
Stop stressing.
Just do it. It's not that hard.

It's really not that big of a deal.
I know how you feel. I get scared sometimes too.

Anxiety is very serious and it's not something to joke about. To someone with anxiety, it isn't just 'that easy' and it's not as easy as 'just go do it'. To someone with anxiety, every little thing can be hard to do and hard to get through. Instead, talk to them. Help them through their panic attacks and help them get to a safe point where they can stop feeling anxious and overwhelmed. Don't say you know how it feels. If you do not have anxiety, then you do not know how it feels.

Don't say these things to someone who is suffering from an eating disorder:

Just eat.
You look so skinny, what's wrong with you?
Look at you, it's gross.
You look so sick.
Have you seen your therapist lately? Look at you.
Why do you keep throwing up? What's wrong with you?

Have you considered going on a diet? That might solve your issues.
Just eat something. It's not that difficult.
Why is it taking you so long to get over this?

Eating disorders are very serious. Don't make comments on how someone looks. That will only make them feel worse. They are still beautiful even if they have an eating disorder. They can and will get better and they are strong enough to realize that they are beautiful just as they are. It just takes time. Take it easy on them.

Don't say these things to someone who self harms:

Stop being so dramatic.
You're only going to hurt your skin. Just get over it already.
You have no good reason for doing that.
What did you use to cut?
Why would you do that to yourself/make yourself ugly?
Can you cover that up with long sleeves? I shouldn't have to see it.
You only do it for attention.
Whatever. It's your body, not mine.

It's just a way of coping, I guess. There's nothing wrong with it.

Self harm is very serious. Telling them to stop won't make them stop. They already know they're hurting their skin, that's the point of cutting, so you don't need to make that comment either. Instead, talk to them about ways they can stop cutting like writing on their skin or using a rubber band. Most importantly, do not judge them. Judging a self harmer will only make them want to self harm more. They know that it's not healthy and they know they need to stop, but they don't know how. That's where you can help them.

Section 38
Distracting Yourself From Pain

I get asked this question multiple times a day and it really depends all on the person. I'm going to talk a little bit about what you might want to try to take your mind off of things...

- Music: Music helps me alot and I know it helps a lot of other teenagers as well. Certain songs can boost your happiness, but even sad songs can sometimes make you feel connected to the song so it might make you feel more understood about what you're going through. I'm also a musician so I'm constantly writing new music and practicing it. If you can do this, do it! It really helps with calming you down from panic attacks.
- Drawing: Draw some pictures or even just a bunch of lines and shapes. It really helps calm you down and it takes your mind off of things and puts it on your drawing. You don't have to be good

at it, just draw whatever you can. It also helps relax the muscles which is good after anxiety attacks.
- Writing: This is the one I use the most. Write about what you're going through. Tell a story. Write about your friends, or your favorite tv show, or your day. Anything. Even if you don't like writing, try it! I always used to hate writing. Now I write pages of inspirational work everyday (thanks Mr. Lambert!).
- Walking/Hiking: I do this alot. Walking and running really helps me through times of stress. I'll go on a 45 minute run in the evening and I will just clear my head from everything. It's really helpful to me.

Section 39
Reaching Out For Help

There's so much help out there if you need it. There's dozens of support websites and there's dozens of support hotlines if you are in a time of crisis. Don't be scared to reach out for support and for help. It's what we are all here for. I'm going to list some resources for you so you can get help regardless of what you're going through.

In any type of emergency, you can always call 911. Don't be scared to call 911. Police, Fire, and EMS are always here to help you. Remember, it's always better to be safe then to be sorry.

The National Youth Internet Safety and Cyberbullying Task Force, Inc. promotes safe online practices for teens, families, and educators. It also serves as a catalyst for the prevention of teen suicide, bullying, teen dating abuse, and human trafficking through education, resources, support, and helplines. The task force is a human services organization and non-profit organization under the Internal Revenue Service's 501(c)(3) tax exemption code.

Executive Director
Alexander J. Kovarovic

Phone Number: 1-844-SOS-ISCB (767-4722)
Email: info@nationalyouthiscbtaskforce.org
Website: www.nationalyouthiscbtaskforce.org

Section 40
Resources

National Youth Internet Safety and Cyberbullying Task Force

Main Phone Number: 1-844-SOS-ISCB (767-4722)

Bullying and Internet Safety Assistance: Extension 0

Teen Suicide Prevention: Extension 1

Dating Abuse Intervention Team: Extension 1

Sexual Abuse Prevention: Extension 3

Social Media Problems: Extension 4

National Resource Center: Extension 5

Email: info@nationalyouthiscbtaskforce.org

Website: www.nationalyouthiscbtaskforce.org

National Suicide Prevention Lifeline

1-800-273-8255

https://suicidepreventionlifeline.org

The Trevor Project

1-866-488-7386

https://www.thetrevorproject.org

National Eating Disorders Association

(800) 931-2237

https://www.nationaleatingdisorders.org/

Crisis Text Line

Text HOME to 741741 from anywhere in the United States, anytime, about any type of crisis.

https://www.crisistextline.org/

Rape, Sexual Assault, Abuse, and Incest National Network

800-656-HOPE (4673)

https://www.rainn.org/

National Domestic Violence Helpline

1-800-799-7233

https://www.thehotline.org/

The Childhelp National Child Abuse Hotline
1-800-4-A-CHILD (1-800-422-4453)
https://www.childhelp.org/

Planned Parenthood
https://www.plannedparenthood.org/

National Hotline for Missing & Exploited Children
1-800-843-5678
http://www.missingkids.com/home

National Runaway Switchboard
(1-800-786-2929)
https://www.1800runaway.org/

National Hotline for Crime Victims
1-855-4-VICTIM (1-855-484-2846)

Section 41
Final Advice

In reality you won't always succeed at everything you try, however that doesn't mean you should stop trying at something. Follow your heart and never give up on your dreams.

Don't try to make everyone like you. It will never work. Even if you do everything right in your life, there will still be someone who says you are doing it all wrong. They could be jealous, insecure, or just simply not like you for whatever reason. Don't take it to heart as it probably has nothing to actually do with you.

Find what you enjoy in life and stick with it. If you enjoy soccer then become the star player. If you want to be a doctor, then do not give up until you're a doctor.

It is always okay to be single. So many of us think it's awful and embarrassing to be single. In reality it isn't that bad. Don't date someone just because you don't want to be alone. Loneliness can be scary, but safety is the main priority. Only date people you feel loved by and comfortable around.

If someone told you a secret, keep it as a secret. Telling other people the secrets your best friend told you will only cause lots of middle school or high school drama.

If you need help, ask for it. Don't be scared for help. We all need help sometimes. There is a lot of people out there to help you through life.

Do not ever lie to your parents about your grades. Sorry guys, they will still find out and you will just be in bigger trouble :(

Always think before you speak or act. Words and actions can hurt others so make sure you use your brain before you start spitting out things you'll regret later.

Try to stick to a schedule during the school year. It may seem stupid, but it will cause you less stress if you know what's going on each day of the week. Plus you won't miss any basketball practices either!

Don't go spending all your money on something you won't use more than a couple of days.
Listen to what your teachers say. You may learn a thing or two.

Alcohol should be taken very seriously. It isn't just something teens do at parties. It's a very serious thing that can have serious consequences. The same goes for drugs.

It is always okay to not want to have sex or sexual contact with others during your teen years. So many teens think it's weird to not have sex while being a teenager. In all honesty, it's a good decision to wait until you meet the right person and until you feel comfortable doing it. Don't have sex just because he wants it or because "everyone else is doing it."

Life doesn't always go as planned. Sometimes change is good.

Talk to an adult about learning to manage your money. That way you won't be broke when you're nineteen.

Don't hate yourself because you made a mistake. We all make mistakes everyday and that's normal. Don't hate yourself for it, just fix your mistakes.

Don't listen to what people say about you. Only you know the real you. What others think won't matter past high school plus they are all irrelevant. Don't spread rumors. They never make you look good.

Never compromise your personal safety or well being for someone else. Do not go into a situation feeling unsafe. If you feel unsafe, get out of that situation now.

Never, ever give less than your best on anything that you do.

Even when it seems like the loneliest time of your life, you are still not alone. There's always someone out there even when you don't believe it.

Always try even when it seems better and easier to give up.

Don't cheat on your boyfriend or girlfriend. This one seems kind of obvious, but yet so many people still seem to struggle with it.

Move on from people that have hurt you, but do not ever forget the lessons that they taught you.

Never forget the people that were always there for you. Those are your true friends and family.

You are always enough. And you are always good enough for others. Don't think down on yourself. You are beyond good enough.

Respect is not easily earned. Do not expect respect when all you do is treat others like dirt.

Don't lose who you are in a relationship. Dating is great, but if it is changing who you are then you may not be with the right person.

Realize and learn the abuse warning signs so you won't ever get taken advantage of or abused in a relationship.

Stay true to who you really are.

The people you think will always be your best friends may drift away from you. That shows who your real best friends are.

It may be rough now, but tomorrow is always a new day.

You learn something new everyday. In reality, you never stop learning.

All the kids in high school that you think are cool and popular won't always be that way. Being popular and cool in high means nothing in the real world.

Think before you fall. People aren't always who they say they are.

Don't wish your life away. Live every moment like it's your last. Do what you love.

Money won't always make you happy. Love yourself and learn to be self confident!

If you want something you've never had, then you've got to do something you've never done.

Opportunity + Preparation = Success

Never forget that even in your darkest times, there is still people that care about you.

Stop living in the past and look at the present. It truly does always get better.
Put school before dating and relationships. Don't worry about dating more than your grades and your health.

Enjoy the simple things in life. You only get to experience them for a short amount of time.

Live in the now. Leave the past in the past and grow from your experiences.

Sometimes it's okay to put yourself before others. Your happiness matters the most so don't forget that.

Don't pass the opportunity to do and try new things.

Nothing great lasts forever if you don't put any effort into it.

Suicide is never the answer. Even in your darkest days, there still is a light at the end of the tunnel. Sometimes it's just a very dim light.

Conclusion
You Can Do It

I understand that it's tough. The hardest part of my depression was the loneliness. No one was ever really there for me. My family didn't understand what was going on with me and they would get very angry with me. My friends all got sick of me and would leave, even after they promised never to do that. I've learned over the years that just because someone states they'll never leave you doesn't mean that they won't. But that's okay. If they decide you aren't worthy of their time then that's their loss. You're being the best person you can be and eventually someone will come along and see how amazing and how strong of a person you are.

You cannot live your life based on how other people feel it should be lived. If people leave then they were never truly worthy of your time, love, and attention. True friends and family will never leave you, even if you're struggling to find out who you really are and where you really belong. Since I was sixteen, only two friends have stayed in my life the entire time.

Throughout my entire life, only one person has always been there for me and I'm honestly fine with that. Even now, I don't tell the people in my life when I win an award or go on tour or speak at a school, because I know the reactions will always be something like "That's nice Alex". I know the people in my life love me, but sometimes it's hard to see it, especially when you're just begging for attention because you feel lonely.

I felt inspired. I wanted to make a difference. I wanted to get stronger. I began wanting to help other people. It became the only thing in my life that truly made me feel like I was worth it. I never felt like I had a purpose for living. I eventually found my purpose. I wanted to kids and teenagers from feeling how I've felt. If I could help just one person then it's worth it to me. I know that when I speak at a school, I won't help everybody. Some people won't even listen to me talk, but if one person goes home and decides that they want to keep living so that they can find their purpose in life then it's all worth it to me.

I still have bad days, sometimes lots of them. Depression, anxiety, eating disorders, and abuse doesn't just go away. It takes time to heal and it's okay if you struggle along the way. You don't have to prove yourself to anyone but yourself. Be happy in your own skin and love all of the accomplishments you make.

Any situation can be worked through, even if it seems like there's no way that it could possibly get better. Nothing is worth your life. Your life's way more important than you see right now. It's okay to feel broken. No one is perfect. Life can be hell sometimes, but don't throw in the towel and give up.

If I gave up a couple years ago, I would never become the person I am today. When I was seventeen I felt that my life was worthless and like it would never get better. I felt that I would never be happy, that it would be better if I just committed suicide so everyone would be happy with me gone. I didn't realize that the pain would pass and that the loneliness would eventually get a lot easier to deal with. But at the time, you don't think about the future. You just automatically assume that you'll still be depressed and that typically isn't the case. If you reach out for help, you can get help so that you can work through your problems. Don't feel embarrassed either, you have nothing to be ashamed of. When I was cutting my skin, I never thought that I was worth much more than that. I thought that seeing my skin bleed would get rid of the pain and in reality, it really didn't. Always know that you're beautiful and worth it, no matter who tells you that you aren't.

Life truly does get better. Even in your darkest days, it will get better. People ask me daily why I do what I do and how it feels to do it. I honestly do it just to help other people, so they don't end up going down the wrong path. I wanted to die and I was willing to do anything to to stop feeling the pain that I was feeling. I want teenagers, kids, and young adults to love themselves just because they are who they are. I want teenagers to realize that they don't deserve abuse, heartbreak, manipulation, and to be put down by the people that claim to love them. I want every teenager to feel comfortable in their own skin, rather than harm themselves because they feel like they worthy of someone else. I want to change lives.

If I have learned anything over the years, it's that you do matter. Suicide does not solve the problems in your life. It only causes pain for others. You may feel like no one cares, but there is someone out there that would question their life if you took your own. It's hard to hear it sometimes, but you do matter and you will make a difference in this world if you just hold on a little longer. The key to life is believing in yourself. Any guy can give you a compliment, and any girl can make you feel good about yourself, but you have to believe in yourself or it's meaningless. You can't expect someone else to love you before you've learned to love yourself. I have many insecurities like I stated earlier, but it's all about embracing them and learning to love yourself the way others do. The key to success is never giving up. Anything is achievable if you fight hard enough for it. Keep fighting and if someone doesn't believe you can do it, prove them wrong. Be unstoppable.

Confidence. I love this word. It has a strong meaning but it's something that can be very hard to have. If you feel self conscious about your appearance or about your personality in general then you need to find out why that is. You were made you for a reason. Don't waste your whole life away trying to be as good as someone else. You are you. People's opinions of you should not matter because they are what I just said, opinions. We all have them. They are totally free to express their opinion, but it doesn't mean that it's right. People may believe it, but only you know the truth and that is all that could ever possibly matter. Opinions, rumors, and judgements are not what make a person. Love, kindness, and respect are what make a person.

"The longer I live, the more beautiful life becomes."
-Frank Lloyd Wright

Many people didn't think I'd be successful at what I wanted to do with my life. Very few people have stuck with me through everything that I've been through and that's okay. I know who my real friends are and that's what a lot of teenagers need to figure out.

I want to thank each and every person who has supported me throughout my journey thus far. Thank you to everyone who has helped me through my depression and through all the struggles I've been through the past few years. I've met some great people throughout my life and I'm beyond grateful for every person that I've crossed paths with.

To everyone who never believed in me, thank you. You pushed me harder everyday. You made me want to become a better person and you helped form the person I am today. You may not have believed in me and you still might not, but that's okay. I have learned to only worry about how I feel about myself.

And lastly, thank you to everyone who has come and gone in my life. Some of you hurt me, some of you taught me lessons, and some of you just decided to leave, but all of you had an impact on the person I've become today, so thank you. To the ones who hurt me, thank you. I am sorry that you chose to do what you did, but I became a better person because of it, so thank you.

Don't give up on yourself. I'm proud of you for hanging in there and I'm proud of you for continuously fighting when it may seem easier to just give up.

"It does not matter how slowly you go, so long as you do not stop." -Confucius

Change your life...

To hire Alex as a speaker or to request to purchase a mass quantity of books for a school or youth group, please email him, message his team on Facebook or Instagram, or reach out by calling the task force at

1-844-767-4722. Alex travels to all fifty states and helps schools purchase his book so teens can be educated even furthur!

Facebook
Alexander Kovarovic

Instagram
@alexanderkovarovic

Email
akovarovic@nationalyouthiscbtaskforce.org

Website
www.alexanderkovarovic.com
www.nationalyouthiscbtaskforce.org

Made in the USA
Middletown, DE
06 April 2019